Contents

KU-825-807

School of Nursing
& Midwifery

Planning Small Scale Research

A Practical Guide for Teachers and Students

K. M. EVANS   BSc MA PhD
Formerly Reader in Education,
University College, Cardiff

NFER-NELSON

Published by The NFER-NELSON Publishing Company Ltd.,
Darville House, 2 Oxford Road East, Windsor, Berkshire SL4 1DF

First Published 1968 by the NFER Publishing Company Ltd.
Revised Edition 1978
Third Edition published by NFER-NELSON, 1984
Reprinted 1985
© K. M. Evans, 1968, 1978, 1984
ISBN 0-7005-0677-2
Code 8184 02 1

Typeset by Illustrated Arts Ltd, Sutton
Printed in Great Britain by Antony Rowe Ltd, Chippenham

Distributed in the USA by Taylor & Francis Inc.,
242 Cherry Street, Philadelphia, PA 19106-1906.
Tel: (215) 238 0939. Telex: 244489.

Preface to the First Edition

At the present time, more people than ever before are engaged in educational research. Many are practising teachers or students in institutes and colleges of education, who have had little or no training in research but who wish to carry out small scale inquiries among their own pupils. The aim of this book is to describe some of the possible types of research and to give a little guidance on how to approach them. It is a book for absolute beginners, and is based upon many years' experience in directing the work of students. Some of the advice offered may seem obvious and elementary, but there is nothing which it has not been necessary to say at some time to some student. In a sense, my students have provided the material, and I am grateful for what they have taught me and glad to be able to pass it on to other, similar students.

The main object of this book is to provide a practical introduction to research of a type which a teacher or student might be able to carry out in a school. It is not concerned with large scale inquiries, which require resources beyond the reach of most individuals. Neither is it intended to be an exhaustive guide to all types of educational research. Obvious omissions are research into the history of education and its philosophy, and comparative education, in which the educational practices and systems of different countries are studied. These, and other types which may spring to mind, are just as truly research as the types discussed, but because their methods and content are so different from those of the experimental work with which this book is mainly concerned, their treatment is omitted. This should not be taken to imply any doubts about their value, but only an appreciation of the limits of what can be contained in a short handbook of this nature.

Another point worth noting is that it will be necessary to read this book in conjunction with a simple textbook of statistics, and suitable works are suggested in the text. Most educational research of the types discussed requires the gathering and manipulating of statistics. The work may be very simple, needing no more than the counting of heads or the drawing up of a table, or it may involve the application of quite advanced techniques of analysis, but anyone starting on a research project should be prepared to acquire any statistical skills needed for its completion. Those not prepared to do this should consider some other type of research, perhaps choosing historical or philosophical topics instead of experimental work.

The actual working out of results is laborious, but the work can be lightened by the use of a calculating machine, where one is available. Many schools now use simple hand machines in arithmetic and mathematics lessons, and they are not difficult to operate. Institutes of education are also likely to have machines which their research students may use, and these may be either hand machines or electrically-operated. The more complicated the machine, the more sophisticated are the tricks it will perform, but even the simplest machine is likely to give valuable help with numerical work.

Where there are no mechanical aids to hand, four-figure logarithms will usually give sufficiently accurate results, and it does not take long to learn to use them. It cannot be stressed too strongly that a knowledge of at least elementary statistical procedures and the ability to carry out the necessary calculations are absolutely essential for experimental research in education.

In conclusion, I should like to express my thanks to all those who have contributed, in one way or another, to the writing of this book. My debt to my research students has already been mentioned. More directly, the officers of the National Foundation for Educational Research have advised me during the preparation of the text, and I should like to acknowledge particularly the guidance I have received from Mr B. S. Cane, Mr A. E. Sanderson and Miss M. Cox. In spite of their efforts, it is too much to hope that the book will contain no matter calling for adverse criticism, but the author alone must be held responsible for any faults which the reader may discover.

K.M.E.
Cardiff, 1968

Preface to the Third Edition

In the years since this book was first published in 1968, changes in the organization of the educational system and developments in the tools of research made desirable first a second and now a third edition. What is surprising is the minor nature of most of the alterations needed.

The 1978 second edition took note of the increase in the volume of educational research and the greater sophistication of the statistical procedures which the general availability of computers made possible. This third edition takes cognizance of more recently published results of research by up-dating references to articles in journals. It also includes bibliographical details of books on methodology written since the earlier editions first appeared.

At the same time, it must be remembered that beginners in research still need to acquire the tools of their trade and that they, like their predecessors, still have to solve some relatively simple problems. It is hoped that this edition will help them to do just that, and at the same time lead them to acquire the skills needed for tackling some of the more complicated questions inherent in the study of a modern educational system. For help in preparing it, I am indebted to Mr A. Yates, former Director of the NFER, and to Miss Veda Dovaston of the NFER-NELSON Publishing Company. They are not, however, to be held responsible for any errors which may have escaped detection, and for these I alone, as author, accept all responsibility.

K.M.E.
Cardiff, 1984

vii

1
Introduction

In the years since the end of the Second World War, probably no development in the field of education in this country has been more significant than the great increase in interest in educational research. Long-accepted principles are being questioned and the demand is growing that they shall be tested. Whatever the present generation of parents takes for granted, it is not prepared to assume without question that local authorities or teachers necessarily know what is best for its children, or that what is provided is always the best. Evidence is required in support of educational practice and theory. Too often, it is felt, practice has been a matter of expediency and theory has been made to fall in line.

The 1944 Education Act, with its provisions for different types of secondary schools, focused attention on the need for more adequate techniques of selection and guidance of pupils at this stage. Research into abilities and aptitudes was a natural result.

Later, the shortage of teachers and dissatisfaction with over-large classes led to the invention of methods of teaching intended to overcome the difficulty. Group and individual methods came into use, and teaching machines and other aids were developed. Inquiries as to the relative effectiveness of different methods of organization and teaching followed.

The result of all this was that more people than ever before engaged in educational research at one level or another, and techniques of inquiry became more varied, more sophisticated, and also much sounder than they had been in the past.

A lead in this work, at national level, came from the National Foundation for Educational Research, which, after its inception in 1947, was responsible for the major large scale and long-term inquiries carried out in this country. As well as carrying out research for government departments and local authorities, it established a register of research in progress, and a journal, *Educational Research*, described as 'a review for teachers and all concerned with progress in education'. The major findings of NFER projects are published by The NFER-NELSON Publishing Company, at Windsor, which also sells educational, clinical and occupational tests and advises on their construction and use.

Another stream of research came from the universities. The shortage of teachers led to the establishment, first, of emergency training colleges and then, of a large number of new permanent colleges of education. The demand for staffs for these colleges, qualified not only to teach the subjects of the school curriculum but also to lecture on the principles of education, resulted in the provision by university institutes and schools of education of courses leading to a variety of advanced diplomas and higher degrees in education. Most of their students were experienced teachers, required, as part of the course, to carry out and report small pieces of independent research. The volume of this work increased rapidly over the years, as did also the research undertaken by members of the staffs of institutes and departments of education.

The establishment of the B.Ed. degree has led to undergraduate students being required to produce dissertations similar to, but simpler than, those generally required at postgraduate level. These tend to be on topics relevant to the courses of study being pursued and are often compilations from existing sources. Sometimes they may involve accounts of experimental teaching the students have carried out in schools, and although they do not, as a rule, add appreciably to existing knowledge, they can be of considerable value to their authors.

The nature and purpose of research

The purpose of research is to extend knowledge – not the knowledge of any particular individual or group, but the pool of existing knowledge available to anyone with the equipment to use it. It follows that some activities often described as 'research' should not be so designated. The dissertations or theses required of some teacher-training students would usually fall into this category, since most of them are no more than summaries or compilations of information already existing, though the material may have to be sought and gathered from a number of sources. It is true that the students do have to search for the information, but since it is available and does not usually involve any independent inquiry on their part, they do not add to existing knowledge and are only studying their topic, not conducting research into it. This is not to decry the value of such work, but only to suggest that it should not be claimed to be other than it is. Its true value lies in the mastery it enables a student to gain over his own subject and the resulting increase in his own knowledge. This is an excellent way of studying a subject, but it is not research.

Usually, genuine research is begun because someone has asked a question and set out to discover the answer. Partial answers, or answers of doubtful truth may already have been given, and further research may be needed to supply a more complete or accurate answer.

Research may involve venturing into areas of thought about which little is known, or it may only involve filling in gaps in existing knowledge. It may necessitate the devising of an experiment or inquiry to be carried out on a nation-wide scale, or only a small investigation in one school or even in one class of a school. If the aim is to increase the extent of our knowledge, or to make it more complete, then research is being done.

Research may also be done in order to test a hypothesis which, as a result, may be either retained or discarded. To discover that it is untenable may be as useful as to confirm that it is true. In either case, knowledge has been extended.

Research is not all of equal value. Sometimes the results may lead to a change in educational policy over a wide area. Sometimes they may lead to changes in methods of teaching particular subjects, such as reading or elementary mathematics. Such results are more likely to stem from large scale projects than from the efforts of individuals, but small scale research can also be of value. An individual worker may produce a test which can be used later by others, or carry out an inquiry which sparks off further and more far-reaching research. A teacher who investigates a new method of teaching his own subject may inspire others to try it, and so improve practice in the schools.

The teacher-training student who gathers material for an elementary dissertation learns a good deal about the topic, but he also learns how to search for information, how to assemble and present it, and how to interpret the findings. These are skills which he will be able to use in other situations and to pass on, in turn, to his own pupils.

The higher degree candidate who carries out an educational experiment learns to analyse his problem, to investigate its background, to apply appropriate research techniques, and to arrive at, appraise and write up the results. At this level, research is often an exercise in the use of methods and a contribution to the education of the student. If it also improves his skill as a teacher, or gives him greater insight into the problems he meets in his own work, so much the better.

It is not easy to tell what research is likely to be of value in the long run. A further extension of knowledge may make a result of extreme importance which seemed useless when first obtained. At the same time, it is neither sane nor honest to embark on research which may use the time, effort and money of many besides the researcher, unless one believes that the results will have some value. Sound work is not likely to be done by a person who has no faith in his own research. What is needed is a sense of proportion.

Probably very few people would make the mistake of assuming that research is easy in any subject, but some appear to assume that results are obtained, with little effort, by the light of brilliant flashes of inspiration. There may be instances where this is true, but advances are far more often made as a result of hard work, and staying power and single-mindedness are very necessary qualifications in a research worker. When the first glow of enthusiasm has faded, dogged determination has carried many a student through to the successful completion of his research.

Patience is another very necessary quality in anyone engaged in educational research. The subjects are human beings, not inanimate matter. They have wills of their own and the capacity for independent action, which may nullify the best-laid research plans. Once this has happened, no further use can be made of a particular group, and it is as well to guard against possible accidents, as far as this can be done, at the planning stage. Failure to do this may necessitate postponing, or even abandoning, the work. A chemist can take another test tube and start again. Another class of children is not so easily come by.

Then, too, the growth and development of children cannot be hastened, and it is often necessary to wait for the appropriate moment to make observations. This is obviously true with studies of long-term development, but experiments involving teaching methods may be spread over as much as a school year, and these often have to be begun and ended at given times during the course.

It must always be remembered that schools do not exist to provide material for higher degree theses. Their only purpose is the education of children, and this must not be hindered without good cause. No-one has the right to demand opportunities for research in a school or college, although most heads and principals are very willing to help serious students when they can. They are, indeed, remarkably kind in this way, whether the applicant is a member of the school staff or an outsider.

Permission to carry out research must always be obtained in advance of starting it, and nothing should ever be done without the knowledge and consent of the head and any other members of staff who may be affected. It is often necessary to get the permission of the Chief Education Officer for the area also. Consultation with the head will decide how the application should be made, and for a member of the staff of a school this is not likely to present much difficulty.

Students who are not members of staff are in a different position. Their research should never be undertaken without the knowledge of the class teachers and heads of the schools, and it should be planned under the guidance of their tutors, who should be in a position to advise on the steps to be taken.

It is both unwise and discourteous for an outsider to make arrangements for research in a school without first obtaining the consent of the local authority through its Chief Education Officer. Often, he will suggest suitable schools and make the necessary approaches to them if the student's needs are explained.

Even when all precautions appear to have been taken, trouble can arise because parents or children resent questions which are being asked in the course of an investigation, and it is not unknown for questions about the activities of research workers to be asked in Parliament. An imaginative and tactful approach should prevent unpleasantness, and submission of proposed questionnaires to the head may prevent the asking, through ignorance of local conditions, of questions likely to provoke unfortunate reactions. Most heads know what can safely be asked in their own schools and colleges.

Finally, a research worker must be honest. It can be tempting to twist results to make them fit a cherished theory, but this must never be done. Results obtained should be considered critically, though it is never easy to be completely objective about one's own work.

Research involves asking a question, and the answer must not be decided in advance. What it will be must depend on the evidence obtained, and 'No' is just as much an answer as 'Yes'. The important point is that the answer should be true. *On the evidence obtained, this is not a tenable theory* is a perfectly satisfactory conclusion to a research designed to test a hypothesis. It clears the way for setting up a more satisfactory theory on which better educational practice may be based.

2
Types of Research

The types of research open to small scale workers are as varied as the people undertaking them. Which is chosen will depend on the interests and personal equipment of the researcher, and on the opportunities for research available to him. A teacher in a school is well-placed to carry out a small inquiry into the effects of his own methods of teaching, or the characteristics of his pupils. Most teachers, at some time or another, look at the class in front of them and wonder 'why' or 'if'. This is the starting point for research, which may involve experimental work in the classroom or may be based on a study of the pupils' school records.

It would be a mistake to assume that educational research is always experimental. Surveys of various kinds and observations of individuals or groups in their ordinary settings can often be carried out successfully by teachers and students.

A survey of literature

Almost any piece of research should begin with a survey of existing literature in order to find out and assemble what is known about a particular topic. When this has been done, it may be found that the original question has been answered and there is no need to go any further.

If the question is not answered, such a survey will give the researcher a thorough grasp of the problem and as complete a knowledge as possible of the existing situation. He is then, and only then, in a position to formulate a hypothesis and design a sound experiment to test it. It is the height of folly to begin designing research without first making a thorough study of the background in this way.

A survey of literature may be done at any level, from the elementary to the scholarly, depending on the qualifications of the researcher and the library resources available to him. It involves a search, not only of books, but also of journals in which research findings are published and discussed, such as *Educational Research*, the *British Journal of Educational Psychology*, *Educational Review*, *New Education and Programmed Learning*, *New Era*, *New Society* and their American counterparts. This is a necessary preliminary to any piece of experimental research, and the student who has learnt to do this has acquired a useful technique. Many examples of research reviews are to be found in *Educational Research* and references to a selection of these follow. The journal itself may be consulted for others.

BURSTALL, C. (1978). 'The Matthew effect in the classroom', *Educ. Res.*, **21**, 19–25.

PRESLAND, J. L. (1980). 'Educating "special care" children: a review of the literature', *Educ. Res.*, **23**, 20–33.

BADGER, M. E. (1981). 'Why aren't girls better at maths? A review of research', *Educ. Res.*, **24**, 11–23.

ROBINSON, C. G. (1981). 'Cloze procedure: a review', *Educ. Res.*, **23**, 128–33.

MOORE, P. J. (1982). 'Children's metacognitive knowledge about reading: a selected review', *Educ. Res.*, **24**, 120–8.

ORNSTEIN, A. C. (1982). 'The education of the disadvantaged: a 20-year review', *Educ. Res.*, **24**, 197–211.

Nearly any educational topic can be followed up in this way, and this is a very suitable exercise for teacher-training students, who do not usually have either the opportunities or the knowledge required for experimental work. By carrying out a survey of the literature they are laying a foundation on which they can build later, when they are better equipped to do so. A student who makes such a survey should end with a thorough knowledge of one educational topic, and, if properly written up, the material gathered in this way can be of use to other students and teachers.

A good college library can usually supply sufficient material to start the researcher on his quest. When its resources have been exhausted, the local university or institute of education library may be able to provide more, and any of these can call upon the aid of other libraries through the inter-library loan service. The Library and Information Services of the National Foundation for Educational Research can often supply bibliographies on selected topics or suggest possible sources of information.

At a quite different level, a survey of literature may be the starting point for independent thought and the development of a new theory. The analysis and synthesis of a large body of material, drawn from many different sources, calls for considerable intellectual power and may be of more practical value than many of the items it covers. From time to time, it is necessary that someone should sit down and make such a survey, in order that research may be planned so as to extend knowledge and not merely reduplicate work which has already been done satisfactorily. At this level, a survey of literature may truly be described as research, and it is in quite a different category from the kind of compilation referred to earlier.

A survey of educational practices or opinions

A survey of literature requires the use of printed sources and can be carried out without the aid of other people. A survey of practice or opinion is a different matter. This involves finding out what other people are doing or thinking and asking them for information. The inquiry might be aimed at finding out what methods of teaching, for example, reading or subtraction, were in use in schools in the neighbourhood, or it might be concerned with the extent to which various methods of classroom organization were being used, or what parents and teachers thought about them. There are many possibilities, as will be seen from the following examples taken from *Educational Research*.

GHUMAN, P. A. S. (1980). 'Punjabi parents and English education', *Educ. Res.*, **22**, 121–30.

O'SULLIVAN, D. (1980). 'Teachers' views on the effects of the home', *Educ. Res.*, **22**, 138–42.

BARKER LUNN, J. (1982). 'Junior schools and their organizational policies', *Educ. Res.*, **24**, 250–61.

GALLOWAY, D. (1982). 'Persistent absence from school', *Educ. Res.*, **24**, 188–96.

YATES, J. W. (1982). 'Student teaching: results of a recent survey', *Educ. Res.*, **24**, 212–15.

TAYLOR, G. H. and SAYER, B. (1983). 'Attitudes of teachers towards the 9–13 middle school', *Educ. Res.*, **25**, 71–4.

YOUNGMAN, M. B. (1983). 'Variations between secondary teachers' jobs', *Educ. Res.*, **25**, 52–9.

A survey of this kind involves making contact with people who can supply the information needed. This may be done, in the first place, by letter, but personal contact is likely to produce better results, and, where possible, an interview should be arranged at which the purpose of the research can be explained and questions about it answered. In this way, interest can be aroused, fears allayed, and co-operation gained.

It may be possible to get the information required during the course of an interview, but more often a written questionnaire will have to be used. In either case, precise questions should be asked, and these should be kept to a minimum, since people in a position to answer are often very busy. For this reason, this type of work should not be undertaken without good cause, and it is not suitable research for teacher-training students. Experience suggests that when they embark on this kind of inquiry they frequently ask for information which is quite easily obtainable from published sources, and often they would have been better advised to go to their college librarian for help in finding it.

Because of the demands made on others, those supervising or undertaking a survey should make sure that the value likely to accrue from the inquiries is commensurate with the work involved in answering them. Tutors and librarians should be able to direct students to suitable books and periodicals, and they should learn to make use of the references most authors provide. When an author has provided a bibliography of several hundred titles, it is not necessary to write to him and ask for further references, but it is by no means uncommon for such requests to be made.

Only information not obtainable from published sources should be sought by personal communication, and public bodies and their officials are not likely to be prepared to make it available to all and sundry. Where they do make it available, they may wish to be reassured as to the use to which it is to be put, and a researcher working under the guidance of a university department or institute of education is likely to be regarded more sympathetically than an individual working alone, unless he is of recognized standing.

Where the circumstances justify the use of this method, valuable information can be obtained, but there is a real danger that the sending out of trivial questionnaires is bringing this type of research into disrepute, to the detriment of serious inquiries.

Methods of constructing questionnaires and analysing replies are considered in Chapter 5.

Case studies

Another very popular form of inquiry is the case study, and many colleges of education require their students to make such a study of one child. Data have to be gathered about his home background, school achievement, health record, intelligence level, special abilities and disabilities, personal qualities, interests, relationships with other children and with teachers, and so forth. Close observation of the child's behaviour is called for, and illuminating incidents in which he figures are recorded. On occasion, the results of standardized tests are included.

The danger with work of this kind is that it may degenerate into the mere accumulation of information about a child. It does not become research unless it serves some definite purpose. For example, it may be desired to understand what factors are contributing to a child's failure or outstanding success in reading, to account for his popularity or unpopularity with his classmates, or to discover the ways in which some physical disability is affecting his progress at school. On occasion, a group of students might co-operate in making a set of case studies of a number of individual children to illustrate some theoretical point or to answer a question. Each student might study a child showing some particular characteristic, such as backwardness at school, and, by pooling the results of their observations, the group might acquire a better understanding of some of the causes of backwardness.

Although work of this kind may not be research in the sense of extending knowledge, it can be a valuable exercise in directing students' attention to factors they might otherwise overlook. It can also give some training in guided observation, and encourage the testing of hypotheses rather than the expression of imperfectly supported opinions about pupils. It is a mistake, though, to draw general conclusions from observations of only a small number of children.

In carrying out a case study, simple tests may have to be used and it is useful for students to learn what kinds are available and suitable for use in the classroom. Further information on obtaining and using tests can be found in Chapter 5. Two articles by D. A. Pidgeon in *Educational Research* are useful in this context.

PIDGEON, D. A. (1961). 'The design, construction and use of standardized tests – Part I', *Educ. Res.*, **3**, 89–99.

PIDGEON, D. A. (1961). 'The design, construction and use of standardized tests – Part II: the interpretation of test scores', *Educ. Res.*, **4**, 33–43.

The following also contain useful information:

JACKSON, S. (1968). *A Teacher's Guide to Tests and Testing.* 3rd Edition, 1974. London: Longman.

YOUNGMAN, M. B. and EGGLESTON, J. F. (1979). *Constructing Tests and Scales (Rediguides 10).* University of Nottingham School of Education.

DOLAN, T. and BELL, P. (1980). *Attainment and Diagnostic Testing (Rediguides 5).* University of Nottingham School of Education.

Books which provide useful accounts of methods of studying pupils, either individually or in groups, are:

GORDON, I. J. (1966). *Studying the Child in the School.* New York: J. Wiley.

WALKER, R. and ADELMAN, C. (1975). *A Guide to Classroom Observation.* London: Methuen.

NISBET, J. D. and WATT, J. (1979). *Case Study: a practical introduction to the methodology of case study in the social sciences (Rediguides 26).* University of Nottingham School of Education.

Used as part of a wider research project, case studies can provide material to illustrate or test a theory, and they may add to the interest of a dissertation and help to humanize what, without such additions, might be an arid statement of observations or facts. Research which has been reduced to mere statistics can seem very remote from the flesh and blood world we know, and case studies, judiciously used, can reclothe the bare bones so that we recognize their relationship to the pupils before us. Many reports use case studies in this way, and examples may be found in the following works:

BARKER LUNN, J. (1970). *Streaming in the Primary School.* Windsor: NFER. (Available from NFER-NELSON).

BLATCHFORD, P. *et al.* (1982). *The First Transition.* Windsor: NFER-NELSON.

NEWSOM REPORT. GREAT BRITAIN. MINISTRY OF EDUCATION. CENTRAL ADVISORY COUNCIL FOR EDUCATION (ENGLAND) (1963). *Half our Future.* London: HMSO.

The most obvious danger of this kind of work is that the case studied may not be typical. It is the unusual child who is most likely to attract attention and to provide the most recordable material, but the extent to which he is abnormal can be assessed only against a good background knowledge of normal children and their behaviour.

Another danger is that a child who is being studied may know it and behave abnormally as a result. It is best if children are not given any inkling that more than usual interest is being taken in them, otherwise they may oblige with the kind of behaviour they think most calculated to impress. Most of them are not above pulling a teacher's leg when it can be done with impunity.

It is possible, also, that either the child or his parents may see a case study as an invasion of privacy, and a sharp division should be made between a scientific study, or one with an educational or therapeutic objective, and an inquiry that is merely aimed at satisfying curiosity.

If a case study is going to be of any value, it must be undertaken in some depth. Some made by students may be very superficial, with little possibility of deciding to what extent they are fiction. A case study in depth is likely to call for more knowledge than many teacher-training students possess, but this is not to say that they should not be encouraged to look at pupils as individuals and try to understand the influences to which they are subjected, both in and out of the classroom.

For the teacher who is a member of a school staff, the position is a little easier. Information about individual pupils builds up when one is in contact with them for a long period, and a teacher who is responsible for a child is justified in asking questions when necessary. This is for the child's benefit, and is not likely to be resented when it is seen in this way by the child and his parents, although the same questions from a student or outsider might provoke complaint. It is as well to consider one's own probable reaction to some personal questions when embarking on work which entails delving into children's personal and private matters.

Sociometric study of a group

The sociometric study of a class or group of pupils often appeals to students and teachers because of its obvious usefulness. Most of us teach pupils in groups, not individually, and an understanding of the relationships between them makes class organization easier. At the simplest level, knowing which pupils are friends and whether any are enemies can help a teacher to promote peaceful relations and reduce friction. Observation of the class at work and play will provide a good deal of information, but if more detailed knowledge of class structure is needed, a sociometric test will help.

Basically, this consists of asking the children who they want to have as companions for particular occupations, and who they do not want as companions. The results can be tabulated or plotted as a sociogram, which shows the relationships and groupings diagrammatically.

If the reasons for particular groupings are to be understood, other information about the children may be needed. The kind of questions that may arise are: *Do the children who live in the same neighbourhood choose one another as friends? Are the children in any one group of a similar level of ability? What common interests draw children together in a group?* Research with a sociometric basis may be extended to cover questions of this kind, and it can also be used in studies of leadership and isolation within a given group.

The journal *Sociometry* provides a wide range of research articles, and the following books and articles are likely to be helpful to beginners in this field.

EVANS, K. M. (1962). *Sociometry and Education*. London: Routledge & Kegan Paul.

EVANS, K. M. (1963). 'Sociometry in school – I. Sociometric techniques. II. Applications', *Educ. Res.*, **6**, 50–8 and 121–8.

HARGREAVES, D. H. (1967). *Social Relations in a Secondary School*. London: Routledge & Kegan Paul.

NORTHWAY, M. L. (1967). *A Primer of Sociometry* (2nd Edition). Toronto: University of Toronto Press.

TOLLEY, H. and THOMAS, K. (1978). *Sociometric technique (Rediguides 18)*. University of Nottingham School of Education.

DAVEY, A. G. and MULLIN, P. N. (1982). 'Inter-ethnic friendship in British primary schools', *Educ. Res.*, **24**, 83–92.

Sociological studies

Another kind of group study is really sociological. It may be desired to investigate the cultural or socio-economic backgrounds of pupils in a school; to find out, for example, whether the children are a representative sample of those in the catchment area, or whether selection is taking place along particular or unintended lines. It has been suggested that some social and cultural groups may be at a disadvantage in school and are less likely than others to go on to further education. A survey might show whether such a hypothesis is substantiated in a particular school.

Again, it might be desirable to find out something about the backgrounds of students taking a particular course in technical colleges or colleges of further education. Some of this information may be available in existing records, and it may be only a question of collecting it together. It might, however, be necessary to gather information from the students themselves, and the remarks made about the use of questionnaires and the making of case studies should be kept in mind. Work of this kind calls for considerable tact on the part of the investigator. Examples of sociological studies will be found in:

TYLER, W. (1977). *The Sociology of Educational Inequality.* London: Methuen.

BALL, S. J. (1981). *Beachside Comprehensive: a case study of secondary schooling.* Cambridge: University Press.

MORTIMORE, J. and BLACKSTONE, T. (1982). *Disadvantage and Education.* London: Heinemann.

STANWORTH, M. (1983). *Gender and Schooling: a study of sexual divisions in the classroom.* London: Hutchinson.

The types of research described up to this point do not involve any experimental work. Instead, they involve observations of pupils or existing situations and the collection of information about them, but without the creation of artificial conditions in the classroom. Frequently, however, educational research involves setting up experimental situations, and consideration follows of experimental research which it may be possible for a teacher in a school to carry out.

Comparisons of teaching methods

One of the commonest types of experimental research is that in which two teaching methods are compared. One class is taught by one method and a parallel class by the other, and the differences in the amounts they have learnt are considered. This involves testing before and after the experimental teaching period and comparing the mean gains in test scores. It sounds easy. It is difficult. And unless stringent precautions are taken, the results are not likely to be very reliable.

It is not easy to get classes which are really parallel, in the sense that each child in one is matched with a child in the other for qualities such as age, sex, intelligence level, and academic attainment. An attempt to match them is likely to disrupt the work of the school far more than the importance of the work usually justifies, and in most cases where such an experiment has been attempted, matching has been less than perfect and errors have, consequently, been introduced from the start.

Other errors creep in because classes are taught at different times, by different teachers, or by the same teacher but not equally efficiently. Because of these and other difficulties, this is not really a good type of experiment for the average beginner in research, although many find it tempting. Those who wish to investigate the methods used in such work will find the following articles useful:

WILLIAMS, J. D. (1965). 'Some problems involved in the experimental comparison of teaching methods', *Educ. Res.*, **8**, 26–41.
GRAY, J. M. (1976). '"Good teaching" and reading progress: a critical review'. In: CASHDAN, A. (Ed). *The Content of Reading*. London: Ward Lock Educational.
BERLINER, D. C. (1976). 'Impediments to the study of teacher effectiveness', *J. of Teacher Ed.*, **27**, 5–13.
GRAY, J. M. (1979). 'Reading progress in English infant schools: some problems emerging from a study of teacher effectiveness', *Brit. Ed. Res. J.*, **5**, 2, 141–57.

Correlational studies

A much more manageable type of research is concerned with the inter-relationships of aspects of the pupils' personalities, backgrounds and attainments. For example, the teacher or student may be attempting to answer the question: *To what extent is progress in a school subject related to intelligence, and do attitudes, interests and home background have any appreciable influence?*

An inquiry of this kind can be carried out on a group of pupils without the necessity of providing a matched group for comparison. It is therefore much easier to arrange than a methods experiment and causes less disruption of the school programme.

This is the kind of research a teacher in a school can carry out, using as subjects a class he normally teaches, or one borrowed for the occasion. It involves, usually, the selection or preparation of suitable tests or questionnaires, their administration to the class chosen, and the statistical analysis of the results.

Examples of studies of this kind can be found in nearly any research journal, but references to three may be helpful in indicating the kinds of inquiries that can be pursued in this way.

SAVAGE, R. D. (1974). 'Personality and achievement in higher education professional training', *Educ. Review*, **27**, 3–15.

ORME, K. (1975). 'Personality, ability and achievement in primary school children', *Educ. Res.*, **17**, 199–201.

BRYAN, P. E. and HASTINGS, B. A. (1983). 'A correlation between O level/CSE 1 grades on entry to an A level course and subsequent A level performance', *Cambridge Journal of Educational Studies*, **13**, 1.

Studies of children's thinking

Another type of inquiry is concerned with the ways in which children reason about various topics, and their understanding of different concepts at different ages. This kind of research has an obvious bearing on teaching methods and on the selection of subject matter for different age groups in schools of all types. Following the work of Piaget, inquiries have been made into the ways in which children think about scientific and mathematical topics, about their own country, about religious ideas, about the issues involved in historical topics, and so on. Sometimes groups of pupils of different ages have been studied; sometimes the same group has been studied at intervals over a period of years. A list of studies of this type follows.

LOUGHRAN, R. (1973). 'Attainment of Formal Thinking as revealed by solving of three-term verbal problems by junior school children', *Educ. Res.*, **16**, 67–73.

LOVELL, K. (1973). 'The development of mathematical and scientific concepts in children', *Educational Development International*, **1**, 23–7.

AUSTIN, K. and JESSON, D. (1974). 'Children thinking', *Mathematics Teaching*, **67**, 37–44.

BURKE, E. (1974). 'Training in logical thinking and its effects on the grouping strategies of eight-year-old children', *Journal of Child Psychology and Psychiatry*, **15**, 303–12.

PAPANDROPOULO, I. and SINCLAIR, H. (1974). 'What is a word? Experimental study of children's ideas on grammar', *Human Behaviour*, **17**, 241–58.

TOWERS, J. D. (1974). 'The development of geographical and spatial concepts and the concepts of country and nationality among 9-year-old Scottish children', *Scottish Educational Studies*, May, 23–6.

POVEY, R. and HILL, E. (1975). 'Can pre-school children form concepts?', *Educ. Res.*, **17**, 180–92.

GUNNING, S. and GUNNING, D. (1976). 'Concepts and thinking skills: teaching strategies in history and social studies', *Education*, 3–13, 43–7.

SKEMP, R. (1979). *Intelligence, Learning and Action.* Chichester: J. Wiley.

MESSICK, S. (1982). 'Cognitive styles in educational practice'. Research report. Princeton, N.J.: Educational Testing Services.

Long-term studies

Most of the types of studies mentioned so far would be classed as 'cross-sectional'. They involve the study of an individual or a group at a particular moment in time, or at two points which are not widely separated, as when a class is tested at the beginning and end of an academic year or term. The results involve descriptions of what the subjects are like *at a particular moment* or estimates of some of the changes which may have occurred in them *between the two points in time at which they were tested*.

Longitudinal studies form a contrast with cross-sectional studies. An individual or a group is observed over a period of time and a record kept of development.

The following are examples of this kind of study:

BARKER LUNN, J. C. (1970). *Streaming in the Primary School.* Windsor: NFER. (Available from NFER-NELSON).

DAVIE, R. (1972). *From Birth to Seven. The second report of the NCDS (1958 cohort).* London: Longman.

BURSTALL, C. *et al.* (1974). *Primary French in the Balance.* Windsor: NFER.
FOGELMAN, K. (Ed) (1983). *Growing up in Great Britain: papers from the NCDS.* London: Macmillan.

Long-term studies of this kind necessitate either prolonged contact with the subjects or access to them at suitable times over a long period. A local authority might follow the progress of children in its schools throughout their school careers, using records obtained for this purpose, or a teacher who remained in one school for a number of years might observe the development of one group of children as they passed up the school.

The value of long-term studies of children's development, physical as well as mental or educational, is undoubted. It is as important to know what a child is likely to become in the future as to know what he is like now, or to know what earlier line of development has made him what he is now. This is not a suitable kind of research, however, for a student who is in a school for only a brief period of school practice, since changes occurring over a short time may be too small to be observed. A student reading for a higher degree or diploma may also find it unsuitable because of the length of time required to obtain sufficient data for a thesis.

Long-term studies in a school or area do, in fact, present considerable organizational problems. The teachers in a school, as well as the pupils, change. New methods of teaching and organization may be introduced. Changes in the catchment area of a school may result in an influx of different types of pupils, or the removal of large numbers of families from the area. In fact, conditions in a school may alter so much over a period of years as to make completion of the work as planned impossible, and the likelihood of this happening should be taken into account at the outset.

All the same, studies of the long-term effects of many educational practices, such as streaming and non-streaming, the use of programmed learning and various kinds of group learning, are needed, and anyone in a position to undertake them should be encouraged to do so. The major projects of this kind, however, are likely to be on a larger scale than an individual worker could undertake and are more suited to the resources of bodies such as the NFER.

3
Preliminaries to Research

Choosing a field of research

Experience of research students suggests that they usually work much more happily on projects they have found for themselves than on those imposed by someone else.

It sometimes happens that there is a question of such burning importance to the individual concerned that no further consideration is necessary, but on other occasions there may be no obvious topic and the student who wishes to carry out research, possibly to fulfil examination requirements, has to cast about for a subject.

When this is the case, it is wise to begin by considering fields of research, rather than specific questions, and to study the chosen field until a specific question can be formulated.

For example, a student might decide to make an inquiry into factors concerned with school failure. Children fail at school at many levels and for many reasons. The field might be narrowed to take account only of children who fail at the O-level of the General Certificate of Education. It might be further narrowed to take account of failure in particular subjects. Then factors which might contribute to failure in these subjects might be considered, and the final question might emerge in the form: *Is X a factor contributing to failure in subject Y at O-level?* X might be an intellectual or personal factor, something to do with home background, interest, something connected with the school, or something quite different from any of these but which appeared to be relevant to the case under consideration.

The choice of fields of research is virtually as wide as the field of education. Possibilities include primary or secondary education, further education, the curriculum as a whole and individual subjects, methods of teaching, attitudes and interests, teachers and pupils. There is no point in prolonging the list. Something can always be added.

In choosing a field, the first consideration should be interest. Work in a field in which one is not interested is irksome and a burden, and little inspiration is likely to result. It is true, however, that work in a field does sometimes stimulate interest. It is not possible to be interested in something about which one knows nothing. For this reason it is wise to choose a field of research about which one already has some knowledge, and for a teacher, his or her own subject or type of teaching will often provide a suitable field. There are always problems and theories about teaching which require investigation, and research into them has a practical, utilitarian value, while facilities for conducting it are usually at hand in school.

This is another important point. It is no good deciding to carry out research if the facilities for it are lacking, or not available to the particular researcher. It is not easy for most teachers to carry out research in schools other than their own, though a lecturer from a university or college of education may be able to gain entry into a variety of schools. Again, research on a foreign school system is usually possible only if one has considerable knowledge of the country in question and its language, and the opportunity to spend some time in the country. Curiosity alone is not a sufficient basis for a research project. There must also be a reasonable opportunity to gratify the curiosity by on-the-spot observation.

Another hindrance to some research projects may be the impossibility of getting permission to carry them out. The need to get permission for any inquiry has already been stressed, and there may be fields of research for which it will not be given. Detailed inquiries into the home backgrounds of children or the characteristics, educational or personal, of their parents, are very likely to fall into this category. Most of us would be justifiably resentful of personal questions from a stranger and suspicious of the uses to which our answers might be put. Children, just as much as teachers, have a right to privacy.

Some useful sources of information

It was emphasized in Chapter 2 that the first step in the intensive study of any field is to find out what work has already been done in it. Titles of all theses presented for degrees in education and educational psychology between the years 1918 and 1960 inclusive are to be found in lists prepared by Blackwell for the National Foundation for Educational Research. More recent titles may be found in the Foundation's lists of current researches, the last of which covers the period up to 1969.

The Aslib *Index to Theses Accepted for Higher Degrees in the Universities of Great Britain and Ireland and the Council for National Academic Awards* contains information about theses in all academic subjects, including education. This publication also gives conditions under which theses may be borrowed from the university libraries where they are deposited. (Published from 1951 onwards.)

The University of London publishes *Theses and Dissertations Accepted for Higher Degrees – Arranged under Boards of Studies with an Author Index*. It covers the years 1929–30 onwards.

Another source of information about recently completed and current research in the United Kingdom is the *Register of Educational Research in the United Kingdom* published by NFER-NELSON. It contains details of approximately 280 bodies including universities, colleges, government departments, institutions and associations. Abstracts are provided where possible and there is an author and subject index. It began in 1976 with the first volume covering 1973–76. There are now five volumes.

Scientific Research in British Universities and Colleges covers the period 1952–75 in three volumes. Volume III deals with the Social Sciences in which Education was first included as a separate heading in 1969–70. *Research in British Universities, Polytechnics and Colleges* is published by the British Library. Volume 3 covers the Social Sciences. It supersedes *Scientific Research in British Universities and Colleges* and appears annually.

Details of theses may also be obtained from *British Education Theses Index* 1950–80. This index is regularly up-dated by supplements and is published as a microfiche.

Research articles should also be consulted. The *British Education Index* gives particulars of articles classified according to subject, which have appeared in a large number of British periodicals since 1954. The *British Education Index* is also available as an on-line service.

Bibliographical details of the above publications follow:

*BLACKWELL, A. M. (1950). *A List of Researches in Education and Educational Psychology. 1918–1948.*

* The *Lists of Researches* by A. M. Blackwell were published for the NFER by Newnes Educational Publishing Co. Ltd., and are now out of print. Copies may be obtained on application to University Microfilms Ltd., St. John's Road, Tylers Green, Penn, Bucks.

BLACKWELL, A. M. (1952). *A Second List of Researches in Education and Educational Psychology. 1949–1951.* London: Newnes Educational.

BLACKWELL, A. M. (1954). *Lists of Researches in Education and Educational Psychology. Supplement 1, 1952–53.* London: Newnes Educational.

BLACKWELL, A. M. (1956). *Lists of Researches in Education and Educational Psychology. Supplement II. 1954–55.* London: Newnes Educational.

BLACKWELL, A. M. (1958). *Lists of Researches in Education and Educational Psychology. Supplement III. 1956–57.* London: Newnes Educational.

BLACKWELL, A. M. (1961). *Register of Current Researches in Education and Educational Psychology· 1959–1960.* London: National Foundation for Educational Research.

NATIONAL FOUNDATION FOR EDUCATIONAL RESEARCH (1962). *Current Researches in Education and Educational Psychology. 1960–61.* London: National Foundation for Educational Research.

NATIONAL FOUNDATION FOR EDUCATIONAL RESEARCH (1963). *Current Researches in Education and Educational Psychology 1961–63.* Slough: National Foundation for Educational Research.

NATIONAL FOUNDATION FOR EDUCATIONAL RESEARCH (1970). *Current Researches in Education and Educational Psychology. 1968–69.* Slough: National Foundation for Educational Research.

ASLIB. *Index to Theses Accepted for Higher Degrees by the Universities of Great Britain and Ireland and the Council for National Academic Awards.* London: Aslib, 1950.

UNIVERSITY OF LONDON. *Theses and Dissertations Accepted for Higher Degrees – Arranged under Boards of Studies with an Author Index.* London: University of London Library, 1929.

NATIONAL FOUNDATION FOR EDUCATIONAL RESEARCH. *Register of Educational Research in the United Kingdom.*

Vol. 1 1973–76. Windsor: NFER. (Available from NFER-NELSON)
Vol. 2 1976–77. Windsor: NFER. (Available from NFER-NELSON)
Vol. 3 1977–78. Windsor: NFER. (Available from NFER-NELSON)
Vol. 4 1978–80. Windsor: NFER-NELSON.
Vol. 5 1980–82. Windsor: NFER-NELSON.
LISE. *British Education Theses Index 1950–80* (plus supplements). Leicester: LISE. (c/o School of Education Library, University of Leicester).
BRITISH LIBRARY. *Scientific Research in British Universities and Colleges. Vol. III Social Sciences.* London: HMSO. (Ceased publication 1975).
BRITISH LIBRARY. *British Education Index, 1954* – London: BLBSD.
BRITISH LIBRARY BIBLIOGRAPHICAL SERVICES DIVISION. *Research in British Universities, Polytechnics and Colleges. Vol. 3 Social Sciences.* London: British Library. Annual.

These lists contain only the titles of researches, not their content, and a student wishing to know how a subject has been treated must look elsewhere for information. Brief abstracts of degree theses are published in some journals, such as the *British Journal of Educational Psychology* and *Educational Research.* Only a limited number of theses can be covered in this way, but a survey of past volumes will give an idea of the kind of work that is acceptable and of some of the ways in which topics have been treated. For fuller information, the thesis itself can be consulted in a library.

Information about published research can be obtained from journals of the type already mentioned, and the review articles in *Educational Research* are particularly valuable. Often, in their summing up, authors direct attention to questions which are still unanswered and in this way suggest further research. Examples of useful review articles have been given in Chapter 2, and many others, dealing with a wide variety of topics, will be found in the journal itself.

Background reading

Before starting on the detailed planning of a piece of research, it is necessary to read as much as possible of the literature already existing on the subject. The search for information is sometimes a problem for beginners, who are usually more used to consulting books than research journals.

Books do not, as a rule, give detailed accounts of research, and their authors are often more concerned with systematizing established results than with assessing the evidence on which they rest. Experimental details are not usually given, but there are often references to original sources which have been consulted in the course of writing the book. These can be followed up.

The author of a book will often express his own opinions, and speculate about aspects of his subject on which little is known. In this way, he may suggest subjects for research, and a critical reader may take up and investigate a point raised.

When using a book in this way, it is wise to look at the date of publication. If this proves to be some years back, there may be more recent work which has altered the whole outlook and which should be consulted. Even if the book is recent, there will have been an interval, probably of at least a year, between writing and publication, and it is not possible for reference to be made in it to research findings published elsewhere in that interval.

Articles in journals can be written and published far more quickly than books, and it is to them that one must turn for the most recent accounts available of research in any field. These articles are usually written by the people who have carried out the work described, and they are therefore primary sources of information. By reading them, one obtains a first-hand account of what was done, how it was done, how the results were obtained and analysed, and what those results were. The soundness of the work may be assessed, and further research may suggest itself.

There are a number of journals which publish fairly detailed accounts of small scale research in education. The most important is probably the *British Journal of Educational Psychology*, but a beginner may find some of the articles difficult because of the statistical nature of the work. It is worth persevering with these, since they demonstrate the kinds of techniques used and help the reader to decide what type of work is likely to be possible in his own case.

Educational Research publishes original experimental work, as well as the review articles mentioned earlier, and this journal bears in mind that many of its readers will be beginners in research. So, too, does the *Educational Review* and some of the other journals published by institutes of education.

These are all British Journals, but there are a large number of American ones which are also worth consulting. Examples would include the *Journal of Educational Psychology*, the *Journal of Experimental Education*, the *Journal of Educational Research*, *Educational and Psychological Measurement*, and *Sociometry*. Different journals deal with different types of work, and the subjects in which they specialize may be discovered by looking through a few numbers of any of those available.

Time may be saved by consulting the *British Education Index*, of which particulars have already been given, and choosing, as a starting point for reading, a suitable article listed there. The American *Psychological Abstracts* is useful too, and this gives outlines of the subject matter of work reported in both British and American journals.

Developments in information handling have been rapid in recent years. Much material is now published in microfilm or microfiche; computerized information banks are also growing fast, and are expected to cover all the major researches carried out in North America and Europe. Specialized facilities are needed in order to use these systems, and students should consult their librarians.

Once one article has been found which deals with the proposed field of research, it is easy to find others. Research workers make use of earlier researches, and any article will contain references to works consulted by the writer. These can be looked up and will, in turn, lead to other articles. In this way much of the earlier published work will be discovered. This reading should be supplemented by a systematic search through back numbers of journals. This may be done either by beginning with the current number and working backwards until a point is reached where no further references to the subject appear, or by starting with some sufficiently early number and working forwards to the current number. This is often dull and hard work and it takes a long time, but it is essential that it should be done if a well-documented piece of research is to result.

When to stop reading can be a problem. Once a series of references has been found, it seems to go on for ever, but after a time further reading does not seem to add to the information already gathered. When that stage is reached, it is time to stop reading and begin planning the experimental work.

Degree theses are also good sources of information. Not only does a thesis give an account of original research, but it also gives references to, and sometimes summaries of, works the writer has consulted.

Conditions under which theses can be borrowed vary from one university to another, and the Aslib list mentioned earlier gives a synopsis of these conditions. Most universities do allow the borrowing of theses, but usually only for reference through the library of another university or college. The difficulty of consulting theses need not be insuperable, and it is worthwhile to make an effort to read a few.

Notes should be taken of all articles and theses read. It is easy to imagine that one will remember their contents, but, in actual fact, so many are usually read that it is quite impossible for anyone with an average memory to dispense with note-taking. It is often very useful to take direct quotations of the more important parts of a work, as in this way the exact result or exact meaning of the writer can be preserved for future reference. Notes, unless they are unduly lengthy, can seem ambiguous when referred to after a lapse of time. Direct quotations included in notes should always be marked as such.

Whenever an article or thesis is read, an exact reference to it should be noted. In the case of an article, this should include the name of the writer, surname first, followed by the date of publication in brackets, the title of the article, the name of the journal in which the article appears, the number of the volume, and the numbers of the pages occupied by the article. An example follows.

BLATCHFORD, P. (1983). 'Children's entry into nursery class', *Educ. Res.*, **25**, 49–51.

The name of the journal is usually abbreviated, and there are standard forms of abbreviation, in most cases, which should always be used. Some of the more important are given later.

In the case of a thesis, the reference should contain the name of the writer, the date when the thesis was accepted, the title, the degree for which it was presented, and the name of the university library in which it is deposited.

THOMAS, K. C. (1981). A study of stereotypes, peer-group friendship patterns and attitudes in a multi-racial school. Unpublished PhD thesis. University of Nottingham.

References to books should give the name of the author, the year of first publication (unless reference is to a particular edition later than the first), the title of the book, the place of publication, and the name of the publisher.

FRANCIS, H. (1982). *Learning to Read: literate behaviour and orthographic knowledge*. London: George Allen & Unwin.

In the examples given, it will be seen that the title of an article is given in quotation marks, but the title of a book or a thesis is not. Internal capitals are used in book titles, but not in thesis or article titles. When written or typed, the title of a journal or book should be underlined to show that, in print, it should be italicized.

It is not suggested that this is the only correct method of giving references. It is given as one method which is in common use, but there are others which are equally acceptable. The main point is to choose an acceptable form and stick to it. Inconsistency in a matter of this kind may suggest slovenly thinking.

It is worth while to take some trouble to note all references accurately, as these will have to be included in the bibliography when the research is reported. References must be given to all work mentioned or quoted, and nothing is more infuriating and time-consuming than having to look these up at the time of writing because they were not noted correctly and fully at the time of reading.

When notes are taken, it is essential to be able to consult them easily at a later date. For this reason, it is better to use a loose-leaf notebook rather than an ordinary exercise book. The loose leaves can be taken out and grouped and re-grouped as required during the course of writing. They can also be arranged in alphabetical order under authors' names to facilitate reference and for making a bibliography. Some people prefer to use a card index, taking the notes on cards with the reference to the author, etc., at the top. These can be filed in alphabetical order and subsequently used in the same way as loose leaves. Whatever method is adopted, much time and effort can be saved by being systematic from the start.

Abbreviations of titles of some commonly used journals

Brit. J. Educ. Psychol.
Brit. J. Psychol.
Educ. and Psychol. Meas.
Educ. Res.
Educ. Rev.
J. Educ. Psychol.
J. Educ. Res.
J. Exp. Educ.
J. Exp. Psychol.

J. Genet. Psychol.
J. Psychol.
Occup. Psychol.
Psychol. Abstr.
Psychol. Bull.
Psychol. Rev.
Rev. Educ. Res.
Sociometry

Formulating a title

After reading some of the background literature, some specific topics within the field may appear to be more interesting than others or to require further research. It is probable that more than one topic will present itself in this way and a choice will have to be made. The determining factors may be the amount of research that has already been done and the possibility of doing more.

When a topic has been decided on, it should be formulated carefully before any research is attempted. An exact form of words for a title should be prepared and, if possible, submitted to a competent adviser. What may seem perfectly clear to the author may be ambiguous to someone who meets it for the first time or who has wider knowledge.

A little latitude in the phrasing is, however, quite permissible and even desirable. The title should not be so precise that it pins the worker down to a very narrow topic or treatment, because, in the course of research, unforeseen circumstances or results can alter the trend of a piece of work and a flexible title allows for this. At the same time, the title should be precise enough to give a real indication of the ground to be covered and, if technical terms are included, they should be used correctly.

If the research is to be submitted to a university for a higher degree, it is necessary to find out the regulations on the registration of titles. Usually, titles have to be approved before the thesis can be submitted, and in many cases there are set dates before which they must be sent in for approval. Failure to comply with the regulations may mean that entry for the examination must be deferred to a later date than was originally intended.

4
Planning Experimental Work

Once the field of research has been chosen and a provisional title decided, the detailed planning of any experimental work involved can begin. The first step is to decide exactly what is being investigated. It may be thought that this will have been done when a topic is chosen, but this is not necessarily true.

Defining the topic

We use a great many terms quite correctly without a precise appreciation of their meanings, and although, in ordinary speech or even in writing, this may not be apparent, it becomes obvious as soon as we begin to carry out research.

Suppose, for example, that the title chosen is *A Study of a Class of Eight-Year-Old Children in a Primary School*. It is probable that this was chosen with a particular class in a particular school in mind, but it still remains to decide how they shall be studied and what information about the children is to be collected. Such a study might involve gathering particulars about any or all of the following:

The social structure of the class
The socio-economic backgrounds of the children
Their scores on an intelligence test
Their reading ages
Their arithmetical achievements
Their attendance records
Their health records
Any evidence of maladjustment or delinquency among them
Their out-of-school interests and activities.

To take another example, suppose that the title is *An Investigation of the Mathematical Ability of Secondary School Pupils*. There are two terms here that need clarification. First, there is the term 'mathematical ability'. This is a complex ability and it is necessary to give the term a precise meaning. A decision must be taken as to what *the writer* means by this term, and this meaning must be stated as precisely as possible and adhered to throughout the research. To avoid adverse criticism, the definition given should be one which will be generally acceptable to people with some knowledge of the subject. The second term needing clarification is 'secondary school'. Here the type of school must be specified, bearing in mind that several types of secondary schools exist.

Another topic may involve an investigation, not of an ability, but of an attitude or other personality quality. Here, a good English dictionary will help to provide an acceptable definition, but a psychological dictionary should also be consulted, so that standard ways of using terms may be adhered to. The coining of new terms, or new meanings for existing terms, should be avoided, as it only causes confusion. The *Penguin Dictionary of Psychology* is a useful book to possess, and this can be supplemented by reference to library copies of more exhaustive dictionaries of psychology.

Choosing the method

When the topic has been defined in this way, it is possible to see more clearly how the research may be carried out, and how the information needed is to be obtained.

The study of the class of eight-year-olds may be based on personal observations of their behaviour and work made by their teacher. Records may be kept of their achievements and progress over a period of time, such as a term or a school year, and notes made of any incidents which seem important. At the end, an account may be written up of their development during the period involved. There would be a large subjective element in such work, since it would depend on the interpretation by the teacher of the children's behaviour in the classroom, and here the experience and objectivity of the teacher would be of paramount importance.

A more objective study would result if standardized tests of intelligence, reading and arithmetic were administered and the scores obtained by the children incorporated in the final report. Indeed, it might be decided to base a whole study on objective tests, and this would probably be the best way to tackle *An Investigation of the*

Mathematical Ability of Secondary School Pupils.

The definition of 'mathematical ability' adopted should suggest what is to be assessed, though not necessarily how it is to be done. Aspects of mathematical ability which might be included would be power of computation, understanding of spatial relationships, and power of abstraction in a mathematical context, and these would then have to be assessed. It is not suggested that this is a suitable or adequate definition of mathematical ability, and the example is used only to give a clearer indication of how to decide what has to be assessed.

Where personal or social qualities are under investigation, it may be necessary to base the research on information supplied about the subjects either by themselves or by people who know them well. Questionnaires, essays and diaries have all been used for this purpose. They are not as objective as standardized tests, but they can sometimes supply data that cannot be obtained in any other way, and their usefulness depends on the skill with which they are used. Questionnaires are so important that they are dealt with separately in Chapter 5.

It is possible to base a piece of research on only one of these methods – observation, tests, or questionnaires – but in many cases a combination of methods is used. Test results may be supplemented by questionnaires, or questionnaire replies checked by observation, or all three methods may be used together. The method chosen is dictated, in part, by the topic, but the predilections of the researcher come into the picture, too.

In some cases, a purely descriptive study might be decided on, such as an account of the activities and conversation of an individual child or a group of children, on a particular occasion or over a period of time. This kind of work is often illuminating and is within the scope of student teachers as well as more experienced workers. Its value depends on the accuracy with which the observations are made and reported and the degree of insight shown in interpreting them.

Research which is not purely observational is likely to involve some kind of educational or psychological assessment, which may entail the use of tests or questionnaires. Deciding what to measure and how to measure it is an important part of a research project, and the selection of suitable tests will be discussed later. First, however, something must be said about the choice of human subjects for the investigation, since any instruments used for assessment must be suited to the subjects with whom they are going to be used.

Choosing the subjects

The subjects of an investigation are the people who are being studied or who are providing the information on which it is based. Often a piece of research is planned with a certain type of subject in mind. It may relate to children in a particular kind of school, to an age-group, to students following a particular course, to members of a Youth Movement or Youth Club, or some other well-defined group. Nevertheless, even when the topic obviously involves one type of subject, the choice of the particular group to be used may still have to be made.

Most people are well-advised to choose subjects of a type with which they are familiar. This makes detailed planning of an investigation much easier, since possible difficulties can be foreseen and evaded. To take an example, the vocabulary of questionnaires must be appropriate to the reading age and comprehension of the subjects, and items which they might find offensive can be omitted or more suitably phrased.

A teacher may find it convenient to use as subjects children he normally teaches, and some inquiries can be carried out in ordinary lesson time without the children realizing that anything unusual is going on. In this way, their normal behaviour is sampled, not something they produce for a special occasion.

If, however, there is any danger that the personal involvement of teacher and pupils may reduce objectivity, it may be better to 'borrow' a class from a sympathetic colleague, or even to obtain permission to carry out the research in another similar school. This is a matter which must be decided by the good sense of the researcher. Sometimes subjects will give information to a stranger whom they expect never to meet again, but hesitate or refuse to give it to someone they know and whom they will have to face again next week.

The question of the number of subjects to be tested is often raised. If the number is too small, the results are not likely to be reliable, but often the number is decided by circumstances. An investigation carried out on a particular class cannot make use of more children than are present in that class. In order to get over this difficulty, two classes in the same school can sometimes be tested, or comparable classes in different schools can be used. In some ways, an experiment of this kind may yield more valuable information than one involving only one large group. Where only one group of subjects is used, we can transfer findings for use only with other exactly similar groups, in exactly similar circumstances. Where several groups are used, we can determine whether the results are suffficiently consistent to be applied to other groups which may vary as much as those originally studied.

More important than the size of the group tested is its representativeness. If a group consists exclusively of boys or girls, it would be unwise to generalize from the results obtained and apply the findings to children irrespective of their sex. So also, results obtained for children of one age should not be taken as typical of children of other ages. If generalizations are to be made on the basis of findings obtained from a small sample of a larger population, care should be taken to see that the small sample matches the larger population in all important respects. For example, the proportion of boys and girls, of children in different age groups, in different social classes, and of different levels of intelligence should be as nearly as possible the same in the sample and the larger population. The extent to which the sample is truly representative should be demonstrated and reported as part of the research.

One thing to avoid at all costs is testing a number of isolated individuals, who may have little in common, and then treating the results as though they had been obtained from one group. However tempting it may be to ask one's friends to help in this way, it should not be done. For one thing, tests given at odd times and in a variety of places cannot be regarded as being given under standardized conditions, and the conditions under which they are given are likely to affect the results.

The answers to questionnaires can sometimes be obtained by sending or giving them to individuals who have something in common, since such people may be regarded as members of a group; from their answers useful conclusions can be drawn about people of their type. This is not on a par with obtaining information from people who may have nothing in common except that they are acquaintances of the person carrying out the investigation. An exception to the rule that isolated individuals should not be tested would occur where the research was in the form of a case study of an individual.

To sum up, the subjects of research should be people to whom the investigator has access, or to whom he can easily obtain access. They should be people with whom he is familiar, or of a type with which he is familiar. In most cases, they should be members of well-defined groups, though there may be occasional exceptions to this rule.

Choosing the tests

Once the research topic has been clearly defined and the subjects to be used in the investigation chosen, it is possible to decide on any tests to be used.

Usually in an experimental investigation, there is one ability or quality which is central to the research and to which others are related. This is called 'the criterion'. In *An Investigation of the Mathematical Ability of Secondary School Pupils*, the *criterion* would be *mathematical ability*, and the test used to measure this would be the *criterion test*.

The criterion need not be an ability; it could equally well be a personality quality. In *A Study of Attitude to Teaching as a Career*, the criterion was an attitude and the criterion test used was a test of attitude to teaching as a career.

The criterion test is the most important one used in any piece of research, and it is essential to see that it is sound. If it is not, the whole research will be invalidated. Points to take into account when forming an opinion about the soundness of a test are summarized in the next chapter. If the criterion test is not valid and reliable, the accuracy of the conclusions reached is bound to be questionable, however good the research design or ingenious the statistical analysis.

Catalogues of tests generally supply information about the groups on which they have been standardized, and this should be taken into account when choosing a test. An obvious factor to consider is the age of the subjects used in standardizing an intelligence test, but such factors as educational level may matter too. Many tests are standardized on students or apprentices or other subjects not really representative of the general population, and the norms supplied may not apply to other types of subjects. Again, intelligence tests are usually standardized on populations which are far more heterogeneous than the average school class, and the results obtained from a small group may be too homogeneous to be useful in discriminating between individuals in it. A test is not usually very useful with subjects who differ markedly from those on whom it was standardized.

Catalogues of tests, such as those issued by NFER-NELSON and other publishers, include a great deal of information about the tests listed which is helpful in distinguishing between those likely to fit the inquiry under consideration and others less suitable. These catalogues merit serious study by anyone undertaking experimental research in education.

Some less technical factors must also be taken into account when deciding what tests to use. The time available for the experimental work will decide the maximum length of the tests to be used, since it is impossible to give a test needing an hour for its administration in a forty-minute lesson period. In assessing the time required, sufficient must be allowed for giving out and collecting scripts, as well as for the working of the tests.

Ease of administration should be considered, especially if tests are to be given by people with little experience in this field. The instructions should be as clear and simple as possible so as to prevent mistakes. A test wrongly administered is valueless, and a mistake may destroy a whole project, especially if it involves the criterion test. Results of another test might be dispensed with in an emergency, but without the criterion measure nothing can be done.

Then, the suitability of the tests for the subjects to whom they are to be administered must be considered. In particular, the age, intelligence and educational level of the subjects must be taken into account. Group tests are not usually suitable for children below about nine years of age. Tests requiring reading and writing are not suitable for people of low ability. People of high intelligence, who are also highly educated, can be very difficult subjects, because they are usually not content to accept questionnaires at their face value, and nearly always criticize them adversely. Also, they sometimes edit tests before answering them, and thus invalidate the results quite as effectively as the low ability reader who fails to grasp what is required of him. The peculiarities of the subjects must always be kept in mind when a method of research is being chosen. If difficulties can be anticipated, they may never actually be encountered.

This applies, too, to the use of questionnaires which may provoke an emotional response. There are some aspects of our lives and personalities which none of us would be prepared to have investigated. This should always be remembered in planning research, and inquiries which might be regarded as offensive should be avoided. It is always possible that permission may be refused for such an inquiry, or that the subjects will refuse to answer the questions asked. A more subtle, but none the less effective, way of queering the pitch is followed by those subjects who, while not overtly refusing to co-operate, give untrue answers. Sometimes the subjects are not fully conscious of what they are doing. Much of the criticism of research which is based on questionnaires stems from doubts about the truth of the information obtained by their use.

The question often arises as to whether it is better to use existing tests or to make tests especially for the particular research. Where suitable tests already exist, it is a waste of effort to make new ones. This is generally accepted in the case of intelligence tests, and unless the research is concerned with the construction of one, no-one would be likely to evolve such a test for a particular experiment. Few people have facilities for making a new intelligence test which would be as good as those already existing.

In the case of personality tests or tests of specific abilities, the position is somewhat different. Many of these tests originate in the USA, and may be less suitable for use in this country than British tests, on account of the differences between the culture, school systems and standards of the two countries. Where American tests are used, results may not be comparable with the published norms. The more frequently used American tests have, however, been 'Anglicized' and restandardized on British populations. Careful attention should be given to test catalogues in order to ascertain whether this has been done.

Deciding how to work out the results

When a piece of research is being planned, it is necessary to decide how the information gathered is to be analysed. Unless this is done, it is quite possible to find, at the end, that because one particular piece of information has not been obtained, only restricted conclusions can be drawn. But for this omission, it might have been possible, with very little extra effort, to have presented a much fuller picture.

If statistical analysis is involved, the techniques to be used should be decided at quite an early stage, and data should be gathered in a form amenable to analysis by the methods chosen. Usually, data which is to be treated statistically should be numerical, or capable of being translated into numbers. For example, if examination results are part of the material to be analysed, they should be expressed as numerical marks. Sometimes, only literal marks or grades are available, and then these may have to be turned into numerical equivalents before any calculations can be carried out. Grades A, B, C, D, E can be replaced by the mid-point marks of the ranges of marks to which they apply. A hypothetical example is given in Table 1. In order to carry out such a conversion, it would be necessary to know what ranges of marks corresponded to the grades used in the actual case involved. The ranges given here are purely hypothetical and should not be taken as universally applicable.

**Table 1: Conversion of Literal Grades to Numerical Equivalents
(Hypothetical Example)**

Grade	Range (Hypothetical)	Mid-point of range
A	90–100	95
B	70–89	79.5
C	30–69	49.5
D	10–29	19.5
E	0–9	4.5

The greatest difficulty is likely to be encountered with material obtained by the use of questionnaires. Answers are often qualitative, and before they can be used statistically they may have to be quantified. In such cases, it is necessary to frame questions so as to elicit replies which can be treated in this way.

For example, instead of asking:

Do you enjoy reading adventure stories?　　　　　　*Yes/No*

it would be better to ask:

How much do you enjoy reading adventure stories?
Very much/Quite a lot/Fairly well/Not very much/Not at all.

The answers in the second case can be translated into scores 4, 3, 2, 1, 0 and by using these, a much truer picture of the taste of the group of children for reading adventure stories can be obtained than if only two classes of response – *Yes* and *No* – were used. The response *Yes* should, if correctly applied, cover all the ratings 4, 3, 2, 1.

Translating qualitative scores into numerical ones in this way involves the assumption that the differences between adjacent pairs of scores are equal at all points of the scale. In the example given, this would mean that the difference between *Very much* and *Quite a lot* is assumed to be the same as that between *Quite a lot* and *Fairly well*, and so on down the scale. Before translating scores and embarking on elaborate calculations, the extent to which this assumption is justified should be carefully considered.

More will be said about this in the chapter on questionnaires. At this point, it is sufficient to warn that a questionnaire may become a trap for an unwary investigator, as it is very easy to gather a great mass of information and then find that one does not know how to analyse it. Probably most research workers have done this at some time in their careers, and it takes quite a lot of ingenuity to deal with the situation. It is much better to think out the problems of analysis at the beginning, instead of resorting to make-do-and-mend later.

Statistical techniques

Far fewer mistakes are likely to be made in carrying out a piece of research if the planning has included a fairly detailed scheme for working out the results, and for this a knowledge of available statistical procedures is necessary. Knowing what can, and what cannot, be done with statistics can materially affect the design of an experiment. It is no use gathering a large amount of information if no suitable procedures exist for treating it. It is also necessary to know what material is required in order to use any given statistical procedure. Anyone wishing to work in the field of educational psychology should, therefore, acquire a sound knowledge of basic statistical techniques, their limitations, and the circumstances in which they may legitimately be applied, before embarking on the detailed planning of experimental work.

For a small scale investigation, a few relatively simple statistical techniques will usually suffice. As a minimum, it is recommended that a beginner should acquire a working knowledge of methods of calculating the mean, the standard deviation, and the coefficients of product-moment and rank order correlation. In addition, he should understand the concepts of 'normal distribution' and 'statistical significance'. These topics are dealt with in elementary statistics books, such as the following. These particular works are recommended because the examples in them are based on educational statistics and they are, for that reason, more directly relevant to educational research than works in which the examples are drawn from other fields.

SIEGEL, S. (1956). *Nonparametric Statistics for the Behavioral Sciences*. New York: McGraw-Hill.
REICHMANN, W. J. (1964). *Use and Abuse of Statistics*. London: Penguin.

BUTCHER, H. J. (1966). *Sampling in Educational Research.* Manchester: University Press.

WISEMAN, S. (1966). *Correlation Methods.* Manchester: University Press.

PIDGEON, D. and YATES, A. (1968). *An Introduction to Educational Measurement.* London: Routledge & Kegan Paul.

YEOMANS, K. A. (1968). *Statistics for the Social Scientist. Vol. I: Introducing Statistics. Vol. II. Applied Statistics.* London: Penguin.

McNEMAR, Q. (1969). *Psychological Statistics* (4th Edition). New York: J. Wiley.

GUILDFORD, J. P. and FRUCHTER, B. (1973). *Fundamental Statistics in Psychology and Education.* (6th Edition, 1978). New York: McGraw-Hill.

CROCKER, A. C. (1974). *Statistics for the Teacher.* Windsor: NFER. (2nd Edition, 1981. Windsor: NFER-NELSON).

Making a pilot study

When the general plan of an investigation is complete, it is wise, if possible, to try it out on a small scale. Perhaps the tests can be administered to a class which is not going to be used in the main investigation, or to a group of children in another school. This is called 'making a pilot study'.

A pilot study serves more than one purpose. In the first place, it gives a chance to practise administering the tests or making the observations. In this way, facility is gained, and the chance of making a mistake which would spoil the whole investigation is decreased. Secondly, it may bring to light any weaknesses in the procedure of administration. Instructions to the subjects can be amended if they are found to be ambiguous or incomprehensible. The time needed for the experiment can be checked. Unsatisfactory methods of recording information can be improved, and generally, the process of testing can be made as simple and foolproof as possible. Thirdly, the statistical procedures can be tried out to make sure they can be applied to the material gathered. Working out the results of the pilot experiment will show whether all the necessary information has been gathered, and they will give some indication of the result to be expected from the main investigation.

The pilot study is not carried out on the same scale as the main study, nor does it necessarily include any retesting, after a period of time, which may be part of the research. It is really a method of testing the procedure to be used, to ensure that, as far as can be foreseen, it is sound, and it may be likened to the testing and servicing of a car by a mechanic before setting out on a long journey.

After making the pilot study it may be necessary to modify the experimental plan, or even to recast it entirely. In an extreme case it may be necessary to abandon the whole inquiry, but this rarely happens if the planning has been done with care. The worst that usually happens is that the main experiment has to be postponed until the difficulties encountered in the pilot experiment have been over-come. This is infinitely preferable to finding out at the end that, because of faulty design, the experiment is valueless. If this happens, there is nothing for it but to start again.

It is a great mistake to be in too much of a hurry over educational research. If work has to be finished by a particular date, then it should be begun well in advance of that date to allow for possible setbacks. It is much better, however, not to try to work to time, but to go ahead steadily with the planning and, when this is complete, to run through a pilot study before the main experiment. A leisured approach, giving time for thought and correction of mistakes, should produce a study which will stand up to criticism in a way that a more hurried one might not.

Settling the details

The last stage in planning an investigation is to go over all the details and make sure that they are as nearly foolproof as possible. It is not possible to foresee all the difficulties that can occur, but many can be avoided.

If an experiment is to be carried out in a school, permission must be obtained from the head and probably also from the Chief Education Officer. The latter is not likely to want to know all the details, but the head should be told as much as possible about the experiment. This courtesy should also be extended to other members of staff, who may help with the project.

The exact time when the experiment is to be carried out should be arranged with the school, and the time it is expected to take should be indicated. It is usually wise to ask for a little more time than is required, to allow for any hitches that may occur. Where testing can be fitted into normal school periods, this should be done, so as to reduce the amount of disturbance of the timetable to a minimum.

Where test material has to be distributed, the method of doing this should be carefully planned. Otherwise there may be a period of chaos at the beginning, and this does not produce an atmosphere conducive to good work on the part of the subjects. Whenever testing is being carried out, a calm and quiet atmosphere should be the aim, and the manner of the person giving the tests will contribute much to this. No matter how important the occasion may be, the person in charge should never fuss or appear over-anxious. The more quiet and matter of fact he can be, the more normal will be the behaviour of the subjects, whether children or adults.

If instructions are to be given orally, these should be prepared in detail. It is not enough to think: 'Oh, I'll just tell them what to do'. The exact wording of what is to be said must be thought out, so as to avoid omitting important points or putting them in the wrong order, and then adding to the confusion by issuing supplementary instructions half way through the session. If more than one person is going to give the tests, or if they are going to be given on more than one occasion, the instructions must be given in a standardized form without impromptu variations.

Where differences between groups are under consideration, it is important to make sure that the data are gathered in such a way that the members of different groups can be discriminated. This is quite easy where the groups are separate classes or in different schools, but it is not always easy when they are subgroups of a larger group. For example, if it is desired to compare the performances of boys and girls in a class, scrutiny of completed scripts will not always indicate which were written by boys and which by girls. Some names, such as Hilary, or Evelyn, do not indicate the sex of their bearers, and there are always some individuals who, when asked to give names, give only initials. Who is to tell whether J. Smith is John or Jane? Thus it is necessary, if differences between groups are to be studied, to make sure that the members of a group can be identified as such without any shadow of doubt. This may seem an elementary point, but this kind of confusion has often occurred.

One point which always has to be decided is whether subjects should be asked to put their names on tests and questionnaires or whether they should be allowed to remain anonymous. Wherever possible, it is better to have their names. Sometimes it is necessary to give a series of tests and, later, to pair the results of one test with those of another. This would be the case when correlational techniques were being used. Sometimes, too, it may. be necessary to bring together test results and information from other sources, such as school records or the results of public examinations. Occasionally, too, a subject has to be asked to make good an omission from a questionnaire. In cases like these, there must be some way of identifying the tests and questionnaires which belong together because they were all filled in by the same person, and it is much easier and more accurate to use names, rather than numbers or any other code. Subjects rarely object to putting their names on tests if the reason for asking them to do so is explained.

Finally, the method of collecting the tests should be planned. If names are required on papers, then a method of checking that they have been put there should be devised. Frequently, subjects will write their name on the first of a set of tests but forget to put it on the rest. If all the tests done by any one subject can be folded together and handed in as a bundle, instead of separately, it is usually easy to identify their writers, even if some of the tests are anonymous. It is very rare for a subject not to write his name on at least one test, and provided he has done this the authorship of the other tests in the same bundle can be correctly ascribed.

5
Tests and Questionnaires

In any research which is not based entirely on personal observation of the subjects, some information is likely to be obtained by the use of tests or questionnaires. These may be administered to individuals or to groups of subjects, and responses may be written down or given orally. The term 'test' is frequently used to include questionnaires, but a distinction can be made by considering the purposes for which they are used.

The *Penguin Dictionary of Psychology* defines a test as 'a standardized type of examination given to a group or individuals; it may be qualitative or quantitative, i.e. determine presence or absence of a particular capacity, knowledge or skill, or determine the degree in which such is present; in the latter case, the degree may be determined by the relative position of an individual in the group or the population, or by assigning a definite numerical value in terms of some selected unit.'

This implies that the object of a test is to discover what a person can do, and the usual method is to require him to answer questions or perform a task and then assess the degree of success with which he does so. We speak of tests of intellectual ability (or intelligence), of arithmetic, of reading, of mechanical skill or aptitude.

The same dictionary defines a questionnaire as 'a series of questions dealing with some psychological, social, educational, etc., topic or topics, sent or given to a group of individuals, with the object of obtaining data with regard to some problem; sometimes employed for diagnostic purposes, or for assessing *personality traits*.'

One type of questionnaire is concerned, not with what a person can do, but with what he has done in the past, or does habitually, what opinions he holds, what he likes or dislikes, what he fears or hopes for, what kind of person he thinks he is.

Another type is more objective, seeking to obtain factual information, perhaps about individuals, about educational practices in a

43

school or an area, or statistics about pupils or the population from which they are drawn.

Responses to a questionnaire may be verbal or numerical and they may or may not be amenable to statistical analysis.

Judging a test

Where tests or questionnaires are used, the success and value of the research is likely to depend on their quality. Results obtained by the use of an unsound test are not likely to be sound, and some criteria for evaluating tests are needed.

The two main qualities to consider are validity and reliability. Briefly, a test is valid if it measures what it is used to measure, and it is reliable if it measures consistently. A test may be reliable without being valid, but it cannot be valid unless it is reliable. It is very much easier to assess reliability than validity, as a rule.

It is important, too, to know whether a test has been adequately standardized and whether the author has supplied norms. These are scores obtained from a representative sample of the population for which the test is intended, and with which scores obtained in the course of the research can be compared.

A very useful discussion of factors to be taken into account when choosing a test will be found in *Essentials of Psychological Testing* by L. J. Cronbach (1970).

The author of any published test should supply with it information about its construction and standardization, as well as evidence of its validity and reliability. There may also exist reports of research in which the test has been used, and from a study of these sources it should be possible to gauge the value of a test and its suitability for the purpose for which it is proposed to use it.

In some cases, research has been done on the tests themselves, and published reports of their characteristics are to be found in journals such as *Educational Research* and the *British Journal of Educational Psychology*.

The most comprehensive single source of information about tests published in English is the *Mental Measurements Yearbook*, edited by O. K. Buros. Other publications reviewing specific kinds of tests (Reading, Mathematics, Pre-school, etc.) are listed at the end of this book. Test publishers' catalogues contain much useful information, although they cannot be expected to be entirely impartial.

Sources of test material

Many tests are published commercially and can be obtained through booksellers or directly from the publishers in the same way as a book or pamphlet. They are not part of the normal stock of the average bookseller, but a shop catering for the needs of students can get them as a special order, if supplied with the details. From a practical point of view, it is better to restrict orders sent in this way to tests published in this country.

The NFER-NELSON Publishing Company holds stocks of many tests, both British and American, and can obtain others on request. Their catalogues repay study. When ordering, it should be remembered that it takes time to get tests not in stock sent over from the United States, and they should be ordered well in advance of the date when they will be needed. Material held in stock in this country can, of course, be obtained much more quickly, but it is never wise to leave ordering until the last minute.

Students wishing to use published tests should study the restrictions on their availability. While many basic attainment tests, such as those produced by the NFER, are readily available to teachers and college lecturers, others are designated as 'closed'. This means that they may be supplied only to Local Authorities, and that they cannot be used without special permission.

Other tests may be supplied only to individuals who are registered as having suitable qualifications. These restrictions may sometimes seem irksome, but they are intended to prevent subtle and complex tests from losing their effectiveness because of overuse, and to protect the person being tested from wrong use and interpretation of the tests.

The range of tests and test publishers is always growing. A list of useful addresses is provided on pages 65–66.

Unpublished degree theses should not be overlooked as sources of test material. Some of these contain tests made for a particular piece of research and give details of their construction, so that it is possible to form an estimate of their value. Permission to make use of these tests must be obtained from their authors, and sometimes from the university to which the thesis was presented, and this permission must always be obtained before using an unpublished test. Usually, it is given very willingly, and the courtesy should be acknowledged in the report of any work in which the test was used. Most authors are very glad to have their tests tried out by other workers, and where possible they should be sent information about the results obtained.

When all available tests have been examined, it may be found that others are required, and these will have to be prepared. This involves learning the procedure of test construction, and it will involve some statistical work. For this, a knowledge of basic statistical procedures will have to be acquired, if not already possessed. A list of works which may be found helpful follows, but it should be added that this is not normally work which should be undertaken by a beginner, and that, where a suitable test exists, it should be used in preference to a home-made one.

Articles

PIDGEON, D. A. (1961). 'The design, construction and use of standardized tests – Part 1', *Educ. Res.*, **3** 89–99.
PIDGEON, D. A. (1961). 'The design, construction and use of standardized tests – Part II: The interpretation of test scores', *Educ. Res.*, **4**, 33–43.

Books

CRONBACH, L. J. (1970). *Essentials of Psychological Testing*. (3rd Edition). New York: Harper & Row.
GULLIKSEN, H. (1960). *Theory of Mental Tests*. New York: J. Wiley.
ANSTEY, E. (1966). *Psychological Tests*. London: Nelson.
TUCKMAN, B. W. (1975). *Measuring Educational Outcomes: Fundamentals of Testing*. New York: Harcourt, Brace, Jovanovich.
NUTTALL, D. L. and SKURNIK, L. (1969). *Examination and Item Analysis Manual*. Windsor: NFER.
NISBET, J. D. and ENTWISTLE, N. J. (1970). *Educational Research Methods*. London: University of London Press.
THORNDIKE, R. L. (Ed) (1971). *Educational Measurement*. (2nd Edition). Washington, D.C.; American Council on Education.
EBEL, R. L. (1972). *Essentials of Educational Measurement*. (3rd Edition, 1979). New Jersey: Prentice-Hall.
DUNN, S. S. (1977). *Measurement and Evaluation in the Secondary School*. Australian Council for Educational Research.
VINCENT, D. and CRESSWELL, M. (1976). *Reading Tests in the Classroom*. Windsor: NFER.

WRIGHT, B. D. and STONE, M. H. (1979). *Best Test Design*. Chicago: MESA Press.

GIPPS, C. *et al.* (1983). *Testing Children: standardised tests in local education authorities and schools*. London: Heinemann Educational.

LEVY, P. and GOLDSTEIN, H. (1983). *Tests in Education*. London: Academic Press.

Drawing up a questionnaire

It frequently happens that, while tests can be found which are suitable for use in a research project, other information is required from the subjects and a questionnaire has to be drawn up in order to elicit it. The information needed may be no more than personal data, such as name, date of birth, sex, home address, school or college attended, and examinations passed. It may, on the other hand, deal with much more complicated matters, such as vocational interests, opinions, and personal adjustment.

The first step in drawing up a questionnaire is to decide its exact purpose, since only when this has been done is it possible to see clearly what information is needed to accomplish this purpose. If this information can be obtained from existing sources, such as school registers, or students' records, there is no need for a questionnaire. If one is necessary, then it should be as brief as is consistent with obtaining all the required information. A long questionnaire is daunting, and may go unanswered where a shorter one would have been filled in cheerfully and returned promptly.

While care should be taken to obtain all the information really needed, there is no point in gathering more than this. To do so lengthens the questionnaire, which is in itself undesirable, and it also makes the work of analysis heavier, since the essential wheat has to be sifted from the non-essential chaff. Most researchers, too, are reluctant to discard any of the information at their disposal, and a good experimental design can be spoiled by unnecessary insertions and appendages. Every examiner knows that a candidate can ruin an answer by giving more information than the question called for, and the same is true of research. The rule should be: Get all the information you need, and no more.

It is worth while to spend a little time thinking out the introductory paragraph for a questionnaire. Even if it is to be given to the subjects by the researcher himself, a brief statement of the purpose of the research, placed at the head of the questionnaire helps to arouse interest and so gain co-operation. More is said in Chapter 6 about the need to do this.

It is very difficult to frame questions which *no-one* can misunderstand, but every effort should be made to see that ambiguity is avoided. A friend may be asked to read the draft through and try to spot possible difficulties, or the questionnaire may be given a trial run with two or three subjects. Quite often, this is sufficient to show up the points where errors are most likely to be made, but even so, a short pilot experiment of the kind described earlier should be made whenever possible.

Answers as well as questions can be ambiguous, and this often means that the question was badly framed. Anyone who asks a child: *Are you a boy or girl?* has only himself to blame if he gets the answer: *Yes.*

A questionnaire is not a test of intelligence and subjects should not have to puzzle out its meaning. The vocabulary should be suited to the people who will be answering the questions, and the wording should be the simplest possible. Double negatives, in particular, should be avoided, as they tend to confuse even the brightest subjects.

The amount of writing subjects will have to do should be kept to a minimum, and adequate space should be left for any that must be done. One useful device is a list of possible answers from which the most applicable has to be chosen, but if this is employed it is necessary to see that the list is as exhaustive as possible. A preliminary trial of the questionnaire will often show whether any other responses should be added, but no matter how careful the inquirer has been there may still be some subjects who wish to give answers not already included. To accommodate these, a space should be left at the end where they can make their own additions.

Providing a list of possible answers is not the same as asking a leading question. The list of answers does not make any one of them appear more acceptable than any other, but a leading question suggests a particular answer is desired or desirable. Makers of detergents may be allowed to ask housewives a question designed to make them express unqualified approval of their product, and 'I like X because it . . .' is a useful commercial advertising gambit. The subject of an educational inquiry, on the other hand, must be allowed to say: 'I don't like X', if that represents his true opinion of X.

It is no use asking questions which the subjects will not answer or will not answer truthfully. No subjects should be asked to supply information which they think could be used to their detriment. Neither should they be asked questions to which they are unlikely to know the answers. In both these categories might come questions put to children about their parents. If the inquirer is a teacher, the children may make up answers rather than admit ignorance or refuse to answer. An inquiry which embarrasses the subjects is pre-doomed to failure because it should never have been made.

Finally, the form and lay-out of a questionnaire should be such that the replies can be analysed as easily as possible. A few mistakes will soon teach the wisdom of this, but a little care taken early will save a lot of time when the work is further advanced. Responses which are dotted all over the page are difficult to score, and wherever possible they should be arranged at one side. As most people are right-handed, it is usually easier for subjects to put answers on the right side of the page, rather than the left.

Multiple choice answers are easier to analyse than open-ended responses, where the subject's meaning has to be extracted before it can be recorded or scored. If the advice given in Chapter 4 about deciding how to work out the results has been followed, fewer unscorable or unanalysable questionnaires are likely to be constructed.

Questionnaires of the type considered above are designed to elicit factual information. The steps in their construction may be summarized as:

1. Define clearly the purpose of the questionnaire.
2. Decide exactly what information is required.
3. Analyse it into its component parts.
4. Frame a series of questions designed to elicit it.

The only qualifications needed for success are the ability to think clearly and to ask plain questions in simple, unambiguous terms.

Questionnaires concerned with habitual behaviour, attitudes and interests require more technical skill, both for their construction and the interpretation of the subjects' responses. Some of them are referred to as 'inventories', and they often resemble tests in that subjects are given numerical scores which enable them to be placed in relation to a pre-determined scale or a designated group. Examples would be the *Eysenck Personality Inventory*, designed to assess neuroticism and extroversion, the *Strong Vocational Interest Blank*, designed to assess suitability for a wide variety of occupations, and the

Study of Values, originally prepared for use in America by Allport and Vernon and now available in a British version by Richardson, which assesses six major attitudes as described by Spranger.

Unless there are unusual research resources available, established tests of this kind are likely to be better than any that a novice in research can produce, and they should obviously be used where appropriate in preference to home-made versions. Information about such tests can be obtained from the major test publishers or from books such as *Personality Tests and Assessments* by P. E. Vernon.

The construction of an attitude test is within the capacity of a beginner. There are a number of ways of assessing attitudes, but the most popular is that originally devised by Thurstone and developed further by a number of workers.

Much has been put into developing attitude and interest tests in recent years. Range, sophistication and variety of techniques have increased sharply, and the beginner is unlikely to need to devise a new test of his or her own, except where attitudes to a specific or local topic are being investigated.

The books listed below contain much useful information on attitude and personality assessment.

EVANS, K. M. (1965). *Attitudes and Interests in Education*. (2nd Edition, 1971). London: Routledge & Kegan Paul.

OPPENHEIM, A. N. (1966). *Questionnaire Design and Attitude Measurement*. London: Heinemann.

TUCK, M. (1976). *How do we Choose? A study in consumer behaviour*. London: Methuen.

RADFORD, J. and KIRBY, R. (1975). *The Person in Psychology*. London: Methuen.

SCHUMANN, H. and PRESSER, S. (1982). *Questions and Answers in Attitude Surveys*. London: Academic Press.

SUDMAN, S. and BRADBURN, N. M. (1982). *Asking Questions – a Practical Guide to Questionnaire Design*. San Francisco: Jossey-Bass.

VERNON, P. E. (1953). *Personality Tests and Assessments*. London: Methuen.

6
The Main Investigation

Carrying out the experiment

Once the experiment has been planned and the tests and question-naires prepared, the actual carrying out of the work is comparatively simple. The arrangements should be made in plenty of time, especially if other people are involved. If tests are to be given in a school, the most convenient time for the school should be arranged. No teacher likes giving up teaching time unless this is unavoidable, and a time near the end of term, after examinations are over, is often best for carrying out testing not connected with school work. When a time has been fixed, it should be adhered to, and this should be quite possible if the research has been properly planned. If the testing is to be done in the investigator's own school in his own lesson periods, there are fewer difficulties over arrangements, but even in this case, the permission of the head should be obtained and he or she should be told when testing is going to be done.

It is most important to secure the goodwill of any subjects who are to be tested, and a friendly approach which sets their minds at rest is best. It should be made clear that their co-operation is appreciated, and they should be thanked for their help. If it is possible to tell them a little about the work and to answer their questions, this should be done. In some cases, it may be possible later to let them know their own test scores, and this is usually greatly appreciated. Of course, no subject should ever be told anything about any individual results except his own.

If testing is to be done by assistants, they should be thoroughly briefed, and should understand both what is required of them and what is being attempted. When all the work has been carried out, any-one who has helped should be thanked and their help should be acknowledged in any report of the work. Schools are usually very willing to give assistance, but they are under no obligation to do so and their courtesy in this respect should not be taken for granted. A note of thanks is a small price to pay for their kindness.

The head of a school and any teachers who have helped with a research project may be interested to know what results have been obtained, and they may find some of the information gained useful to them in their own work. It is difficult to justify the time and effort spent on research if there is no feed-back from it to the schools, and even a small piece of experimental work can sometimes produce usable material. Where a teacher is studying his own pupils and methods, the feed-back is direct, but in other cases it may be necessary to give a short report of the main findings. The decision to use this material or not lies with the head, who can judge its practical value in the school better than anyone else.

Working out the results

As a preliminary to working out the results, any tests given must be scored and other material obtained from the subjects must be sorted out. This is purely mechanical work, but it takes time and it must be done accurately.

When the scripts have been marked, the results should be tabulated, and if this is done clearly it greatly simplifies the work. Experience shows that there are real advantages in tabulating all the information about a group on one large sheet of paper, as shown in Table 3, before carrying out any calculations. In this way it is possible to see whether there are any subjects from whom complete sets of data have not been obtained, either because they spoiled some of their scripts or because they were absent when some of the tests were given. These

Table 3: Test Scores for Whole Group

Names	Test 1	Test 2	Test 3	Test 4

subjects should be eliminated from the inquiry and results calculated only for those for whom the data are complete.

Usually the next step is the preparation of a grouped frequency distribution of the scores for each test. This shows the numbers of subjects whose scores fall in successive intervals of the scale, and an example is given in Table 4.

Table 4: Grouped Frequencies of Scores on Test 1

Interval	Frequency
0–9	5
10–19	13
20–29	19
30–39	11
40–49	9
50–59	6

Sometimes it may be desirable to present a distribution graphically, and a block diagram (or histogram) derived from Table 4 is shown in Figure 1.

Notice that the axes of the graph are labelled to show which variables (scores, frequencies) are represented along them and that both tables and graphs are numbered and titled. Information on constructing tables and diagrams is given in *Statistics for the Teacher* by A. C. Crocker.

It is impossible to over-emphasize the value of a methodical approach to statistical work. If this is set out in an orderly manner, the speed of working is greatly increased, the danger of making mistakes is greatly reduced, and the checking of working is made much easier. As a rule, only the results of calculations are shown in the final report, but this does not mean that the actual working can be done untidily on scraps of paper. To be slovenly over statistics is to court disaster.

The actual methods used will depend on whether a computer or other machine is available. If the calculations are being done without any such aid, four-figure logarithms usually give a sufficient degree of accuracy. This question of degree of accuracy is important, as no results can be more accurate than the measurements on which they are based.

In education and psychology, test scores are usually given as whole numbers, and to carry calculations on them to several places of decimals is quite unjustified. Intelligence quotients are a case in point, and so are examination marks. To give the mean intelligence quotient for a class as 104.3791, or the mean mark in arithmetic as 53.8725, suggests a spurious level of accuracy. In the case of means and standard deviations, the nearest whole number may be all that is really justified, and for correlation coefficients two places of decimals are likely to be the limit. This is a place for the exercise of common-sense, taking into account the accuracy of the data and the use to which the results are to be put.

When measures such as coefficients of correlation or differences between means are stated, their levels of significance should always be given. Briefly, the level of significance denotes the odds that a particular difference or correlation coefficient is not due solely to chance factors. The size of the difference or correlation coefficient which is significant depends on the size of the group to which it refers, and, in general, the larger the group, the smaller is the difference or coefficient which is significant.

For an explanation of the concept of statistical significance, reference can be made to Chapter 8 of *A First Course in Statistics* by E. F. Lindquist. Methods of determining levels of significance are given by Chambers, and also by Daniels and Lewis. The use of statistical tables is involved, and extracts from some tables and instructions for using them are given by all these writers. If the full tables are needed, those by Fisher and Yates, or the newer type by G. H. Fisher, are suitable. Anyone engaged in research should learn how to use such tables correctly.

Figure 1: Distribution of Scores on Test 1

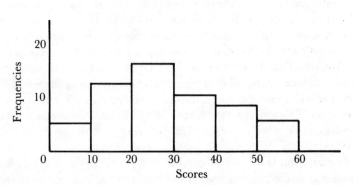

FISHER, R. A. and YATES, F. (1948). *Statistical Tables for Biological, Agricultural and Medical Research*. (6th Edition, 1974). London: Oliver & Boyd.

FISHER, G. H. (1964). *The New Form Statistical Tables*. London: University of London Press. (Second Edition, 1965. Sevenoaks: Hodder & Stoughton.)

Tabulating the results

When the results have been worked out, they should be gathered together and arranged in such a way that they can be easily referred to when writing the report. Here again neatness and orderliness are very important. Numerical results are best tabulated. The tables should be arranged in order and numbered, and each should be headed clearly to show the subject matter. If graphs are given, these, too, should be clearly labelled. There should never be any question as to what figures, diagrams or tables refer to, and a stranger with sufficient knowledge, looking through the results, should be able to understand what was done and what results were obtained.

Tabulation of results is usually fairly straightforward, but sometimes it calls for a little ingenuity. Examples of a few common methods follow.

Table 5 is a straightforward display of means and standard deviations of scores from four groups of subjects to whom Test 1 was administered. Note that the heading makes this clear to the reader.

Table 5: Means and Standard Deviations (Test 1)

Group	No. in group (N)	Mean (M)	S.D. (σ)
A	52	29.3	6.5
B	63	30.6	6.4
C	25	25.4	6.6
D	21	28.6	4.4

When the meanings of symbols, such as N, M, and σ have been established, they may be used as headings for columns in later tables. This has been done in Table 6.

Table 6 is more complicated than Table 5, as it is designed to bring out the differences between two groups on a series of tests. Note the method of using double headings for some of the columns and of sub-dividing columns.

Table 6: Comparison of Mean Test Scores obtained by Groups A and B

Test	Group A			Group B			Diff. of Means	Level of Significance
	N	M	σ	N	M	σ		
1	52	29.3	6.5	63	30.6	6.4	−1.5	Below 5%
2	52	30.4	6.4	63	27.5	6.7	+2.9	5%
3	52	39.0	7.0	63	43.7	5.9	−4.7	0.1%

Correlation coefficients, too, can be tabulated. In Table 7 are shown the coefficients obtained when the scores made by the members of four groups on two tests were correlated.

Table 7: Correlations between Scores on Test I and Test II

Group	N	r	Level of significance
W	22	+0.02	Below 5%
X	28	+0.55	1%
Y	30	+0.39	5%
Z	28	+0.41	5%

If a series of tests has been given to the same group of subjects and the results from each test correlated with those from each of the others, a correlation matrix gives all the coefficients obtained. Table 8 shows the lay-out.

Table 8: Intercorrelations of Test Results (109 Subjects)

Test	Correlation coefficients (r)					
	I	II	III	IV	V	VI
I		0.32**	0.21*	0.21*	0.20*	−0.06
II			0.05	0.06	0.05	0.17
III				0.51**	0.11	−0.13
IV					0.25*	0.04
V						0.25*

* significant at the 5% level   ** significant at the 1% level

It will be seen that, by tabulating results, a great deal of information can be given clearly in a small space. It is wise to prepare tables showing the main results before writing up the research, and arranging them in order so that the discussion can be based on them. In this way, the line of the argument can be laid down. The tables themselves should be incorporated at suitable points in the report where they can be referred to easily by readers.

7
Reporting Research

Students often tend to suppose that writing up a piece of research will not take long. This is a mistake, and ample time should always be allowed for this part of the work. Some of it may be done before the experimental work is carried out, but the main portions cannot be written until all the work, including the calculation of results, has been completed.

The purpose of a report is to communicate the results of research to anyone interested, but this does not mean that the report need not have literary merit. The better the literary presentation, the more surely will the aim of communication be achieved. A good, clear style makes for easy reading, while an awkward or involved style distracts the reader's attention from the subject matter. It should not be necessary to have to disinter an author's meaning from a welter of ill-constructed sentences.

Since much research is reported in degree theses, the writing of a thesis will be considered first.

Writing a thesis

A question often asked is: 'How long should a thesis be?' It is quite impossible to answer this, for the length will depend on the topic and the detail in which it is treated. All one can say is that it must be long enough to ensure adequate presentation of the work but that it should not be artificially lengthened by the inclusion of irrelevant subject matter. 'Padding' will not fool the examiner, and it may irritate him.

The introductory chapter should set out the subject of research, its aims and the proposed method of treatment. This should be done only in general terms at this stage, and the details should be left until later. The introduction should show why the research is considered important and what has led to its being undertaken. The scope of the inquiry should also be indicated.

Following the introduction should come a review of previous researches on the subject and of any other relevant work which has been consulted. Brief accounts of articles and other theses mentioned should be given, compiled from the notes taken when reading up the background of the subject. On the whole, it is better to avoid direct quotations, but if these are used they should always be indicated and the sources acknowledged. They should be kept short, for what is required is not a jigsaw of other people's work, but the writer's own views. Anyone making a serious study of a topic should have opinions of his own about earlier researches, and should resort to statements of the type, 'X says . . .', only if he intends to go on and comment on what X says.

When referring to other people, titles such as Professor or Doctor are omitted and only the surname is used. The form of words used in introducing references should be varied as much as possible, so as to avoid monotony and ensure smooth writing. Phrases such as: 'In a recent report, X states . . .' or 'X, commenting on this point, suggests . . .' are preferable to the bald, 'X says . . .', which, when repeated too often, reduces the reader to asking, 'What do *you* say?'

Proper references should be given to all articles or theses mentioned, and these may be given in footnotes or in a list at the end of the chapter. A better method, however, and one which is much easier for the writer to organize, is to list references alphabetically, according to authors' names, in a bibliography at the end of the thesis. In the body of the text, reference is by author's name followed by the date of publication of the work in question in brackets, e.g. Cattell (1936). This is known as the *Harvard Method*. No work should be cited which has not actually been read by the researcher.

The review of earlier researches can be a difficult part of the thesis to write. The articles cited are usually quite distinct, although they are all concerned with roughly the same topic, and to bring them together into a patterned whole requires considerable skill. Yet this must be done, and it must be shown how the projected research fits into and extends the pattern. The review articles in *Educational Research*, to which reference was made earlier, should be studied as examples of the ways in which discrete research findings can be brought into relation with one another.

The design of the research should be described next, and this must be done clearly, so that the reader knows exactly what was done, and why, and how. The exact tests given must be specified, with reasons for choosing them. If tests have been constructed, the work must be described in detail, though sometimes it is best to do this in a separate chapter, only mentioning the tests at this stage. Copies of all test material used should be included wherever possible, though this need not be done in the case of well-known tests. Often tests are best inserted either at the end of a chapter or in an appendix at the end of the thesis, so as to avoid breaking the thread of the argument. If it seems necessary, examples of items from them can be included at appropriate points in the text.

The subjects of the experiment must also be described. If they are children, the reason for which they were chosen, the type of school they attend, their age, sex and any other relevant information about them should be given. If several groups are used, information about them may sometimes be tabulated.

Finally, the methods employed in working out the results should be discussed. The reasons why they were considered appropriate and their advantages over other possible methods should be mentioned.

This section of the report should be such that, after reading it, anyone who wished could repeat the experiment. If the reader is left with only a vague impression of what was done, then the reporting has not been satisfactory.

After this, reporting the actual experiment is not difficult, but presenting the results is less simple. Where statistical methods are used, they should be indicated, but it can be assumed that the reader will be familiar with standard methods. Only any unusual use of a method need be described in detail, and such a proceeding must be justified. Only researchers with a very thorough knowledge of statistical methods are likely to be able to apply them in ways which are both sound and unconventional, and beginners should stick to orthodox practices.

It is not necessary to include all calculations, but the data on which they are based and the results must be given. Often it is better to give the data in an appendix rather than in the text. Results are better tabulated whenever possible, and ways of doing this have been indicated in Chapter 6.

Tables should be numbered consecutively and they should be headed so that the reader can understand them without having to search through the text for enlightenment. Columns also should have clear headings.

Where it is necessary to show the forms of distributions, diagrams can be used, and these, like tables, should be numbered and titled. In graphs, the axes should be labelled and scales shown. The aim of graphical presentation is to make information clearer than can be done by a list of numbers, and a graph which does not do this fails in its purpose. It is quite permissible to use coloured inks in diagrams, if this serves a real purpose, but colour is not a substitute for clarity and neatness.

Both diagrams and tables should be inserted in the text so that they can be referred to easily. It should not be necessary to search through several pages to find the table or diagram under discussion. If tables or diagrams are too large for easy insertion, they can be made out on large sheets of paper and folded to fit into the thesis itself. If this is done, care must be taken to see that the sheets can be opened out and consulted reasonably easily.

The interpretation of the results should come next, and this is probably the hardest section of the whole thesis to write. The obtained results must be gathered together in such a way as to bring out any pattern there may be. Conclusions must be drawn, and these must be drawn only from the evidence presented and not go beyond it. Discussion of the conclusions is permissible, and applications of the findings and suggestions for possible further research may be indicated. This all calls for great honesty, and there may be a temptation to claim greater importance for the research than is justifiable on the basis of the evidence presented. This is a temptation that must be resisted, whatever the cost.

A summary of the whole work follows, and this should be brief and clear. It is often best to give it in the form of a series of numbered statements. It should give an indication to the reader of what has been done, what results have been obtained, and what conclusions have been drawn. It should never include any new material and it should not be a repetition of earlier sections of the report. The summary is important, since what he finds there may determine whether a reader consults the rest of the thesis or puts it back on the library shelf.

The bibliography should come immediately after the summary, and should contain all the relevant works to which reference has been made in the course of the research. Items should be arranged in alphabetical order of authors' surnames and the forms given in Chapter 3 should be used. Mention will have been made of some of these works in the body of the thesis; others will have been consulted but not specifically mentioned. Some workers divide their biblio-graphies into sections, showing works to which specific reference has been made in one section and other works consulted in another.

The appendix or appendices should complete the thesis. Here should be found copies of all test material used, and any statistical data which it is not convenient to include in the text.

It only remains now to add a table of contents and write a foreword. The foreword should be an acknowledgement of help received and anyone to whom special gratitude is due should be thanked by name. If permission to use copyright material has been given, this also should be acknowledged.

The thesis is now complete and it should be read through as criti-cally as possible. Some passages will almost certainly need revision and some additions or deletions have to be made. Care should be taken to see that one section leads on naturally and easily to the next, and that the argument flows, with no sharp breaks. In fact, the thesis should be welded into a whole.

At this stage, it is useful to ask someone with sufficient knowledge of the subject to read and criticize the thesis. A student working under a tutor will normally have the benefit of the tutor's comments on his manuscript. A teacher working alone would be well advised to ask for help from a member of the staff of his local institute of education before presenting his work for examination, if he has not done this at an earlier stage in his research.

The manuscript is then ready for the typist. Most universities lay down regulations about the format of theses (size of paper to be used, spacing, layout, binding, and so forth), and these should be studied and complied with. The pages should be numbered consecutively by the typist.

The typed copies should be read carefully, and any errors made in copying should be corrected, making sure that corrections are made in *all* the copies of the thesis. Normally, two or three copies have to be sent in for examination, and they must be identical in content.

If the thesis has to be bound, the university will normally supply specifications and sometimes the name of a book-binder who will carry out the work. If binding is not required, the pages must be fastened together firmly, so that the thesis can be opened and read in comfort and does not fall to pieces when handled. It is worth taking a little trouble to find a suitable folder or loose-leaf binder to hold the thesis. After all, it does represent a great deal of time and effort.

Writing an article

Much of what has been said about writing a thesis applies also to writing an article, but there are some important differences. Some of these are due to differences in the types of readers for whom the work is intended.

A thesis is primarily intended to be read by the examiner, and it must therefore demonstrate that the writer has a mastery of his subject matter and a sound grasp of the techniques he has used. The reader of an article in a journal is not so much interested in assessing the writer's competence as in finding out what results he obtained. For this reason an article should be much less detailed than a thesis and the background of the research should be indicated only in broad outline. References to earlier work should be brief, and the main investigation and its results should be described succinctly and clearly.

The summary of an article is very important, and it may come either at the beginning or at the end. This is likely to be read first by most readers, and what they find there will determine whether they read the rest of the article. From the summary, it should be possible to get a clear idea of the research and its results.

An article is usually written for submission to a particular journal, and where this is the case, other articles in recent issues should be studied. Many journals require articles to conform to a given pattern, and one which does not do so is more than likely to be refused by the editor, or, at best, returned for revision.

Points to note are whether sub-headings are used, whether a bibliography is needed, and, if so, in what form references are given. The use of footnotes should be considered, and they should, in general, be brief. If it is found that lengthy footnotes are needed to make the text intelligible or modify statements made in it, then the article probably needs rewriting.

Tables and diagrams should be kept to a minimum. Diagrams, in particular, are difficult and expensive to produce, and some journals require the writer to pay for their preparation. The substance of tables may often be stated succinctly in good prose, but the criterion to use in deciding how to present material must always be that of clarity of expression. The aim should be to present material in the most readable form possible consistent with accuracy and correctness of statements.

Learned journals do not pay writers for articles they accept for publication, but they usually give them a stated number of off-prints of their own articles and the opportunity to buy extra copies for a small sum.

The following publications which give advice on reporting research may be found useful. The pamphlet by Wiseman deserves particular attention.

WISEMAN, S. (1952). *Reporting Research in Education*. Manchester: University Press.

MITCHELL, J. H. (1968). *Writing for Technical and Professional Journals*. New York, London: J. Wiley.

WARD, R. A. (1977). *100% Report Writing*. London: Thames Polytechnic.

FIGUEROA, P. M. E. (1980). *Writing Research Reports (Rediguides 23)*. University of Nottingham School of Education.

Although a good deal of helpful information and advice can be obtained from books, there is never any real substitute for personal effort. The only way to learn to write is by writing, and the only way to learn to do research is by doing it oneself. If you have read as far as this, and want to find out more about educational research, you should now plan, conduct and report an inquiry of your own.

Appendix 1: Sources of Information

Information sources on research

The best source of information on research work currently being undertaken in Britain is: *The Register of Educational Research in the United Kingdom* published regularly by NFER-NELSON for the National Foundation for Educational Research. Other sources of information are detailed in Chapter 3.

Tests

NFER-NELSON publishes three 'open' test catalogues: *The Educational Guidance and Assessment Catalogue; Catalogue of Clinical Tests and Procedures; Catalogue of Tests for Industry and Commerce.* All of these catalogues are up-dated regularly and contain much useful information. They are obtainable on request from:

> The Promotions Department
> NFER-NELSON
> Darville House
> 2 Oxford Road East
> Windsor
> Berkshire SL4 1DF

NFER-NELSON also publishes a range of books and pamphlets reviewing available tests and current issues in testing.

For a more detailed review of reading tests, teachers should consult:

VINCENT, D. *et al.* (1983) *A Review of Reading Tests*. Windsor: NFER-NELSON.

VINCENT, D. (1984). *Reading Tests for the Classroom Teacher*. Windsor: NFER-NELSON.

Other educational test publishers in Britain include:

Hodder & Stoughton Ltd	Macmillan Education Ltd
PO Box 700	Houndmills
Mill Road	Basingstoke
Dunton Green	Hampshire
Sevenoaks	RG21 2XS
Kent TN13 2YA	

Catalogues are available from all test publishers on request.

For a general directory of tests currently available in the English language, consult:

BUROS, O. K. (1978). *Eighth Mental Measurements Yearbook*. Highland Park, N.J.: Gryphon Press.
MITCHELL, J. V. (1983). *Tests in Print III*. Lincoln: University of Nebraska Press.

Appendix 2: Planning Research – Flow Chart

**Preliminaries
to Research**

Theoretical Planning

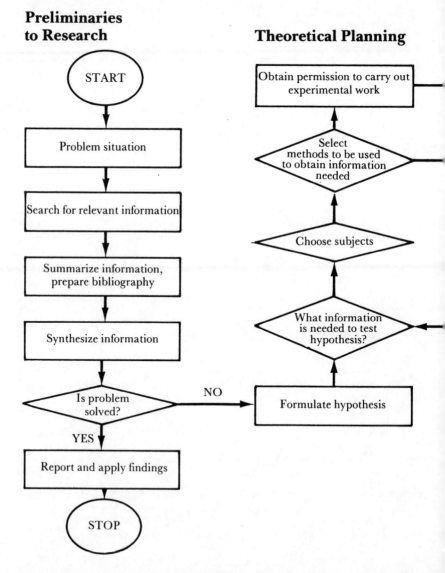

START

Problem situation

Search for relevant information

Summarize information,
prepare bibliography

Synthesize information

Is problem
solved?

NO

YES

Report and apply findings

STOP

Obtain permission to carry out
experimental work

Select
methods to be used
to obtain information
needed

Choose subjects

What information
is needed to test
hypothesis?

Formulate hypothesis

Key:

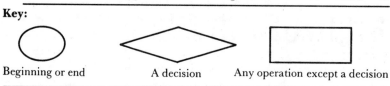

Beginning or end   A decision   Any operation except a decision

Practical Work

Analysis and Presentation

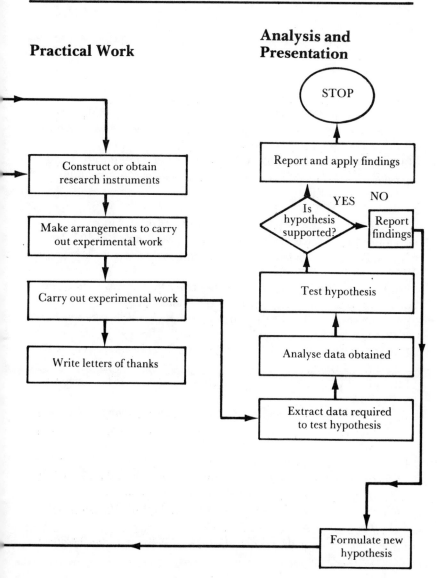

STOP

Report and apply findings

Is hypothesis supported?   YES   NO

Report findings

Construct or obtain research instruments

Make arrangements to carry out experimental work

Carry out experimental work

Write letters of thanks

Test hypothesis

Analyse data obtained

Extract data required to test hypothesis

Formulate new hypothesis

Bibliography

ANSTEY, E. (1966). *Psychological Tests*. London: Nelson.

ASSOCIATION OF SPECIAL LIBRARIES AND INFORMATION BUREAUX. (ASLIB). *Index to Theses Accepted for Higher Degrees in the Universities of Great Britain and Ireland*. 1950–.

BLACKWELL, A. M. (1950). *A List of Researches in Education and Educational Psychology. 1918–1948*. London: Newnes Educational (for NFER).

[The *Lists* by A. M. Blackwell are now out-of-print, but copies are available from University Microfilms Ltd., St. John's Road, Tylers Green, Penn, Buckinghamshire. For complete list see p. 21–2.]

BALL, S. J. (1981). *Beachside Comprehensive: a case study of secondary schooling*. Cambridge: University Press.

BARKER LUNN, J. (1970). *Streaming in the Primary School*. Windsor: NFER. (Available from NFER-NELSON.)

BLATCHFORD, P. *et al.* (1982). *The First Transition*. Windsor: NFER-NELSON.

BRITISH LIBRARY. *British Education Index, 1954–*. London: BLBSD.

BRITISH LIBRARY. *Scientific Research in British Universities and Colleges. Vol. III. Social Sciences*. London: HMSO (Ceased publication 1975).

BRITISH LIBRARY BIBLIOGRAPHICAL SERVICES DIVISION. *Research in British Universities, Polytechnics and Colleges. Vol. 3 Social Sciences*. London: British Library. Annual.

BUROS, O. K. (Ed) (1978). *The Eighth Mental Measurements Yearbook*. New Jersey: Gryphon Press.

BURSTALL, C. *et al.* (1974). *Primary French in the Balance*. Windsor: NFER.

BUTCHER, H. J. (1966). *Sampling in Educational Research.* Manchester: University Press.

CHAMBERS, E. G. (1952). *Statistical Calculations for Beginners* (2nd Edition). London: Cambridge University Press.

CHANAN, G. and DELAMONT, S. (Ed) (1975). *Frontiers of Classroom Research.* Windsor: NFER. (Available from NFER-NELSON.)

COOPER, B. M. (1964). *Writing Technical Reports.* Harmondsworth: Penguin.

CROCKER, A. C. (1974). *Statistics for the Teacher.* Windsor: NFER. (2nd Edition, 1981. Windsor: NFER-NELSON).

CRONBACH, L. J. (1970). *Essentials of Psychological Testing* (3rd Edition). New York: Harper & Row.

DANIELS, J. C. (1953). *Statistical Methods in Educational Research.* University of Nottingham Institute of Education.

DAVIE, R. (1972). *From Birth to Seven. The second report of the NCDS (1958 cohort).* London: Longman.

DELAMONT, S. (1976). *Interaction in the Classroom.* London: Methuen.

DOLAN, T. and BELL, P. (1980). *Attainment and Diagnostic Testing (Rediguides 10).* University of Nottingham School of Education.

DUNN, S. S. (1977). *Measurement and Evaluation in the Secondary School.* Australian Council for Educational Research.

EBEL, M. (1972). *Essentials of Educational Measurement.* New York: Prentice-Hall.

ENGELHART, M. (1972). *Methods of Educational Research.* Chicago: Rand McNally.

EVANS, K. M. (1962). *Sociometry and Education.* London: Routledge & Kegan Paul.

EVANS, K. M. (1965). *Attitudes and Interests in Education.* (2nd Edition, 1971). London: Routledge & Kegan Paul.

FIGUEROA, P. M. E. (1980). *Writing Research Reports (Rediguides 23).* University of Nottingham School of Education.

FISHER, G. H. (1964). *The New Form Statistical Tables.* London: University of London Press.

FISHER, R. A. and YATES, F. (1948). *Statistical Tables for Biological, Agricultural and Medical Research.* (6th Edition, 1974). London: Oliver & Boyd.

FOGELMAN, K. (Ed) (1983). *Growing up in Great Britain: papers from the NCDS.* London: Macmillan.

GIPPS, C. *et al.* (1983). *Testing Children: standardised tests in local education authorities and schools.* London: Heinemann.

GORDON, I. J. (1966). *Studying the Child in the School.* New York: J. Wiley.

GRAY, J. M. (1976). '"Good teaching" and reading progress: a critical review'. In: CASHDAN, A. (Ed) *The Content of Reading.* London: Ward Lock Educational.

GUILFORD, J. P. and FRUCHTER, B. (1973). *Fundamental Statistics in Psychology and Education.* (6th Edition, 1978). New York: McGraw-Hill.

GULLIKSEN, H. (1960). *Theory of Mental Tests.* New York: J. Wiley.

HARGREAVES, D. (1967). *Social Relations in a Secondary School.* London: Routledge & Kegan Paul.

JACKSON, S. (1968). *A Teacher's Guide to Tests and Testing.* (3rd Edition, 1974). London: Longman.

LEVY, P. and GOLDSTEIN, H. (1983). *Tests in Education.* London: Academic Press.

LEWIS, D. G. (1967). *Statistical Methods in Education.* London: University of London Press.

LINDQUIST, E. F. (1942). *A First Course in Statistics.* New York: Houghton Mifflin.

LISE. *British Education Theses Index 1950–80 (plus supplements).* Leicester: LISE c/o (School of Education Library, University of Leicester.)

McCOLLOUGH, C. and VAN ATTA, L. (1963). *Statistical Concepts.* New York: McGraw-Hill.

MITCHELL, J. H. (1968). *Writing for Technical and Professional Journals.* New York, London: J. Wiley.

MORTIMORE, J. and BLACKSTONE, T. (1982). *Disadvantage and Education.* London: Heinemann.

NATIONAL FOUNDATION FOR EDUCATIONAL RESEARCH (1962). *Current Researches in Education and Educational Psychology. 1960–61.* London: Newnes Educational (for NFER).

NATIONAL FOUNDATION FOR EDUCATIONAL RESEARCH (1963). *Current researches in Education and Educational Psychology. 1961–63.* Slough: NFER.

NATIONAL FOUNDATION FOR EDUCATIONAL RESEARCH. *Register of Educational Research in the United Kingdom.* Vol. 1 1973–76. Windsor: NFER. (Available from NFER-NELSON). Vol. 2 1976–77. Windsor: NFER. (Available from NFER-NELSON).

Vol. 3 1977–78. Windsor: NFER. (Available from NFER-NELSON).

Vol. 4 1978–80. Windsor: NFER-NELSON.

Vol. 5 1980–82. Windsor: NFER-NELSON.

NESBITT, J. E. (1966). *Chi-Square*. Manchester: University Press.

NISBET, J. D. and ENTWISTLE, N. J. (1970). *Educational Research Methods*. London: University of London Press.

NISBET, J. D. and WATT, J. (1979). *Case Study: a practical introduction to the methodology of case study in the social sciences (Rediguide 26)*. University of Nottingham School of Education.

NORTHWAY, M. L. (1967). *A Primer of Sociometry* (2nd Edition). Toronto: University of Toronto Press.

NUTTALL, D. L. and SKURNIK, L. (1969). *Examinations and Item Analysis Manual*. Windsor: NFER.

OPPENHEIM, A. N. (1966). *Questionnaire Design and Attitude Measurement*. London: Heinemann.

PIDGEON, D. and YATES, A. (1968). *An Introduction to Educational Measurement*. London: Routledge & Kegan Paul.

RADFORD, J. and KIRBY, R. (1975). *The Person in Psychology*. London: Methuen.

REICHMANN, W. J. (1964). *Use and Abuse of Statistics*. London: Penguin.

SCHUMANN, H. and PRESSER, S. (1981). *Questions and Answers in Attitude Surveys*. London: Academic Press.

SIEGEL, S. (1956). *Nonparametric Statistics for the Behavioral Sciences*. New York: McGraw-Hill.

SKEMP, R. (1979). *Intelligence, Learning and Action*. Chichester: J. Wiley.

STANWORTH, M. (1983). *Gender and Schooling: a study of sexual divisions in the classroom*. London: Hutchinson.

SUDMAN, S. and BRADBURN, N. (1982). *Asking Questions – a Practical Guide to Questionnaire Design*. San Francisco: Jossey-Bass.

SYMONDS, P. M. (1931). *Diagnosing Personality and Conduct*. New York: Appleton-Century-Crofts.

THORNDIKE, R. L. (Ed) (1971). *Educational Measurement* (2nd Edition). Washington, D.C.: American Council on Education.

THURSTONE, L. L. and CHAVE, E. L. (1929). *The Measurement of Attitude*. Chicago: University of Chicago Press.

TOLLEY, H. and THOMAS, K. (1978). *Sociometric Technique (Rediguide 18)*. University of Nottingham School of Education.

TUCK, M. (1976). *How do we Choose? A study in consumer behaviour*. London: Methuen.

TUCKMAN, B. W. (1975). *Measuring Educational Outcomes: Fundamentals of Testing*, New York: Harcourt, Brace, Jovanovich.

TYLER, L. E. (1963). *Tests and Measurements*. New Jersey: Prentice-Hall.

TYLER, W. (1977). *The Sociology of Educational Inequality*. London: Methuen.

VINCENT, D. and CRESSWELL, M. (1976). *Reading Tests in the Classroom*. Windsor: NFER.

VINCENT, D. *et al*. (1983). *A Review of Reading Tests*. Windsor: NFER-NELSON.

WALKER, R. and ADELMAN, C. (1975). *A Guide to Classroom Observation*. London: Methuen.

WARD, R. A. (1977). *100% Report Writing*. London: Thames Polytechnic.

WISEMAN, S. (1952). *Reporting Research in Education*. Manchester: University Press.

WISEMAN, S. (1966). *Correlation Methods*. Manchester: University Press.

WRIGHT, B. D. and STONE, M. H. (1979). *Best Test Design*. Chicago: MESA Press.

YEOMANS, K. A. (1968). *Statistics for the Social Scientist. Vol. I. Introducing Statistics. Vol. II. Applied Statistics*. London: Penguin.

YOUNGMAN, M. B. and EGGLESTON, J. F. (1979). *Constructing Tests and Scales (Rediguide 10)*. University of Nottingham School of Education.

Index